UNGRAFTING

EDITED BY KATJA RIVERA

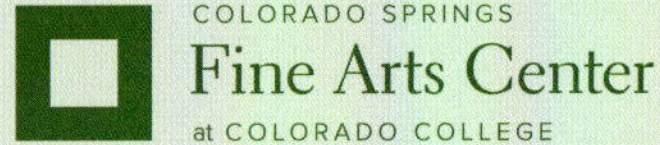

INVENTORY PRESS

UNGRAFTING

HƯƠNG NGÔ

DIRECTOR'S FOREWORD

MICHAEL CHRISTIANO

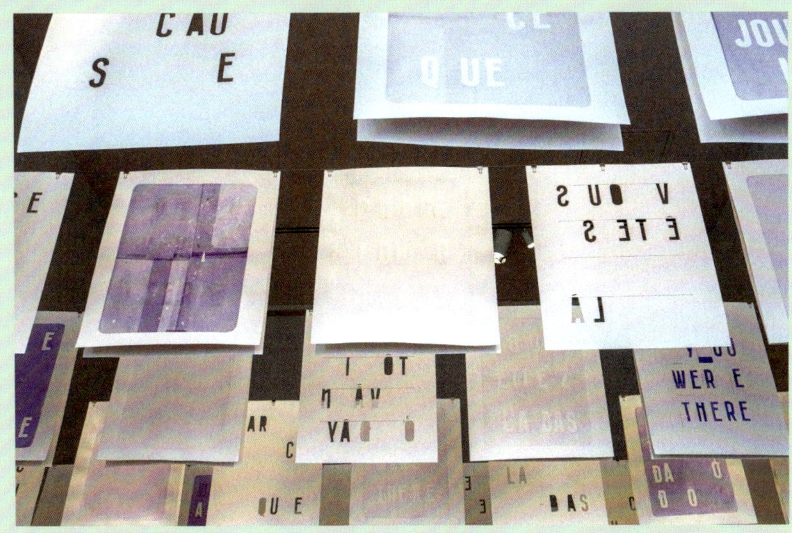

Detail of *We are here because you were there*, 2016–ongoing.

Hương Ngô: Ungrafting continues the Colorado Springs Fine Arts Center at Colorado College (FAC) Museum's ongoing effort to organize exhibitions that resonate with our sense of place. Ngô does this through a rigorous engagement with the history of French colonialism in Indochina (Vietnam, Cambodia, Laos), focusing specifically on the systematic control of plants, agriculture, and knowledge. Impressively, she makes connections between her research and our own region's history by acknowledging a shared struggle for land and resources by Indigenous peoples. We are grateful to her for this project and for engaging with our faculty, students, and broader communities.

Thanks to Colorado Creative Industries for the support of the exhibition. For their important loan, we thank the DePaul Art Museum (DPAM). Thanks also to the FAC's Executive Director, Nicole Herden, for her support of the project. Many thanks to Luke Cammack, Operations Manager, and Mark Cannon, Assistant Operation Manager, as well as the entire Patron Experience Team: Melanie Audet, Kari Bell, Megan Brockriede, Cordelia Colt, Rob Estes Danielle Sanchez, Angie Schwickerath, Tiffany Scott, Darla Slee, and Ian Stewart. This team looks after both the art and our visitors with exceptional care. Thanks also goes to Frances Huntington, Patron Services Manager, and Matthew Driftmier, Patron Services Assistant Manager, for their support throughout the entire run of the project.

Thanks to Katja Rivera, Curator of Contemporary Art, for shepherding both the exhibition and catalogue. The contributors to this catalogue—Chadwick Allen, Evyn Lê Espiritu Gandhi, Aline Lo, and Justin Quang Nguyên Phan—have given voice to *Ungrafting* through their research and writing to offer fertile and intersecting readings that reveal the diverse layers of Ngô's project. I thank them for their insightful contributions. Finally, thank you to the artist Hương Ngô for her unwavering commitment and generosity.

INTRODUCTION & ACKNOWLEDGEMENTS

KATJA RIVERA

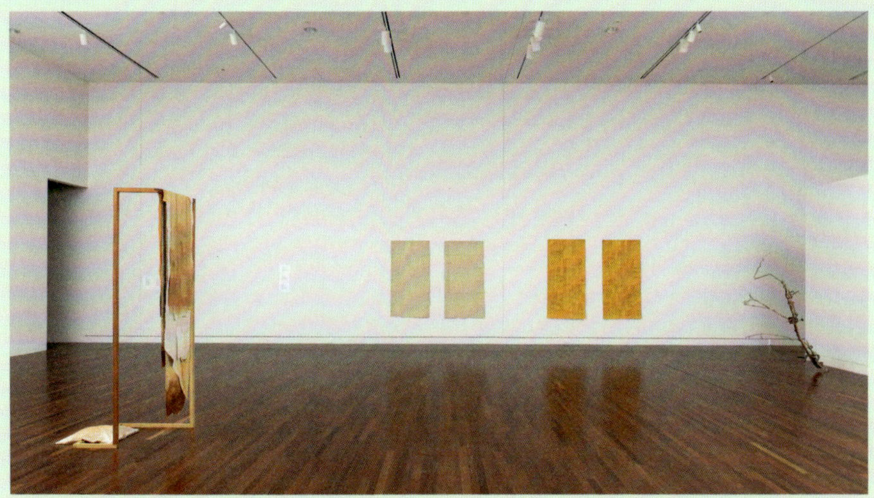

Installation view of *Ungrafting*, Fine Arts Center at Colorado College, 2024.

I first encountered Hương Ngô's work in Chicago, in 2016, and found it to be a powerful example of what it means to be thoughtful. The work was carefully considered; special attention was paid to how materiality connects to content and meaning. Much of Ngô's work emerges from archival research in Vietnam, France, and the United States, which has been beautifully contextualized in this publication by Dr. Justin Quang Nguyên Phan. Rather than presenting us with this research as regurgitation of an official narrative, Ngô manages to draw on it in inventive ways, activating it through imagery, language, and material matter in order to disrupt our perception of history as static, linear, and objective. As she states in her interview with Dr. Aline Lo: "part of my work is to introduce doubt and bring instability into...institutional spaces." She achieves this unsettling, in part, by attending to form and materiality, using photosensitive or even invisible inks; inviting transformation and deterioration into her process; and bringing focus to the act of translation and the passage of time. In all of this, Ngô's intent is not simply to critique but to offer a space for reflection as a way to move forward, thoughtfully.

For her solo exhibition at the Colorado Springs Fine Arts Center at Colorado College, Ngô conceived the term "ungrafting" as a decolonial methodology. Derived from "grafting," a procedure that involves cutting and splicing different species into a single plant, "ungrafting," is an attempt to think poetically about what it might mean to break with the harms documented in (and at times aided by) the historical record. But this break is not a simple smoothing-over, not an elision of past harms. Rather, it operates via the act of troubling, and the scars remain visible. Specifically, rather than seeking to undo histories of violence and colonization, "ungrafting" is Ngô's suggestion for attending to them instead and celebrating resistance and care along the way. In so doing, she allows—as the scholars Dr. Chadwick Allen and Dr. Evyn Lê Espiritu discuss—connections to emerge between places, specifically between French Indochina and the American Southwest, with a particular emphasis on Colorado. In the artist's words, she seeks to "[draw] connections to shared histories in her work." Given my own interest in how many of us are tethered to more than one place or location, I celebrate this gesture and am grateful for it.

Ungrafting began as a conversation in 2020 and there are many people to thank for the realization of this project. Michael Christiano, Director of Visual Arts and Museum, gave his support to the exhibition early on, recognizing the importance of the project for our various communities. Jonathan Dankenbring, Exhibition Designer/Preparator Manager and JD Sell, Museum Preparator, were critical thought partners in the preperation and planning of the installation, lending their keen insights and expertise to every facet of the production. Special thanks also to the team of preparators who supported the installation: Kerstin Brooks and Alix Garcia. Sara Hodge, Head of Collections, and her team—Christian Valvano, Assistant Registrar, and Brittany Hall, Assistant Collections Manager—attended to the works with an exceptional level of care and weathered each variation of the exhibition with good humor. Alana Adams, Assistant Curator of Collections, joined the team just before the opening of the project, but she provided a much-needed enthusiasm and support for the final push, and I am deeply grateful for her research and writing on the works that were featured from the FAC permanent collection. Thanks to Rebecca Rounds, Director of Events, who was a champion of our opening. Blair Huff, Academic Engagement Manager, was supportive of the faculty and students who connected with the exhibition. Stormy Burns, Administrative Assistant, remained consistently unflappable and provided critical support, for which I thank her sincerely.

In addition to the museum team, many people contributed invaluable time and work to the success of the project. Jessi Burns, Marketing and Communications Strategist, was instrumental in getting the word out about this exhibition, and for her support I am extremely grateful. Sarah Waddell, Communications Specialist, lent her enthusiasm and smart ideas to every phase of this project.

Special thanks go to the contributors to this publication, who have shared their words and ideas to not only articulate the importance and meaning of Ngô's work but also to expand the conversation in order to explore the shared resonances that ripple across discrete disciplinary methodologies. Justin Quang Nguyên Phan has contextualized Ngôs long engagement with archival research throughout her artistic practice. He brings a sharp and focused reading of the works in *Ungrafting,* elucidating exactly how science and agriculture becomes a tool for military and imperial control, and beckons us to not only see but also listen to the works. Aline Lo conducted an insightful interview with Ngô that tackles tough questions about the possibility and challenges of work that engages with a historical archive and the construction of colonial knowledge. Finally, Chadwick Allen brought his conceptualization of the "trans-Indigenous" into conversation with Evyn Lê Espiritu Gandhi's expertise in refugee studies to explore how *Ungrafting* attends to two disparate places: Vietnam and the US. Together, these two scholars think through the movement, translation, and connections that are revealed as a result.

For the thoughtful design of the book, I thank Adam Michaels and V.E. Chen from Inventory Press who brought a keen eye and a collaborative spirit to the project. Zoe Kauder Nalebuff kept us all on track, and this book would have not been completed without her. Thanks also to Eugenia Bell, a wordsmith who generously contributed her expertise. Thanks to Forgotten Shapes, Hương Ngô and Giang Nguyễn for providing type for the book. We were fortunate to work with the photographers Stacy Platt, Jonathan Dankenbring, JD Sell, and Wes Magyar, who translated the exhibition into images for this publication.

Finally, I would like to thank Hương Ngô. I am honored that she entrusted this project to me and the FAC Museum team. Many thanks to her for being such a generous, patient, and deeply engaged collaborator. For allowing us all to see and listen to the world, and its interwoven histories, through her eyes and ears, I am especially grateful.

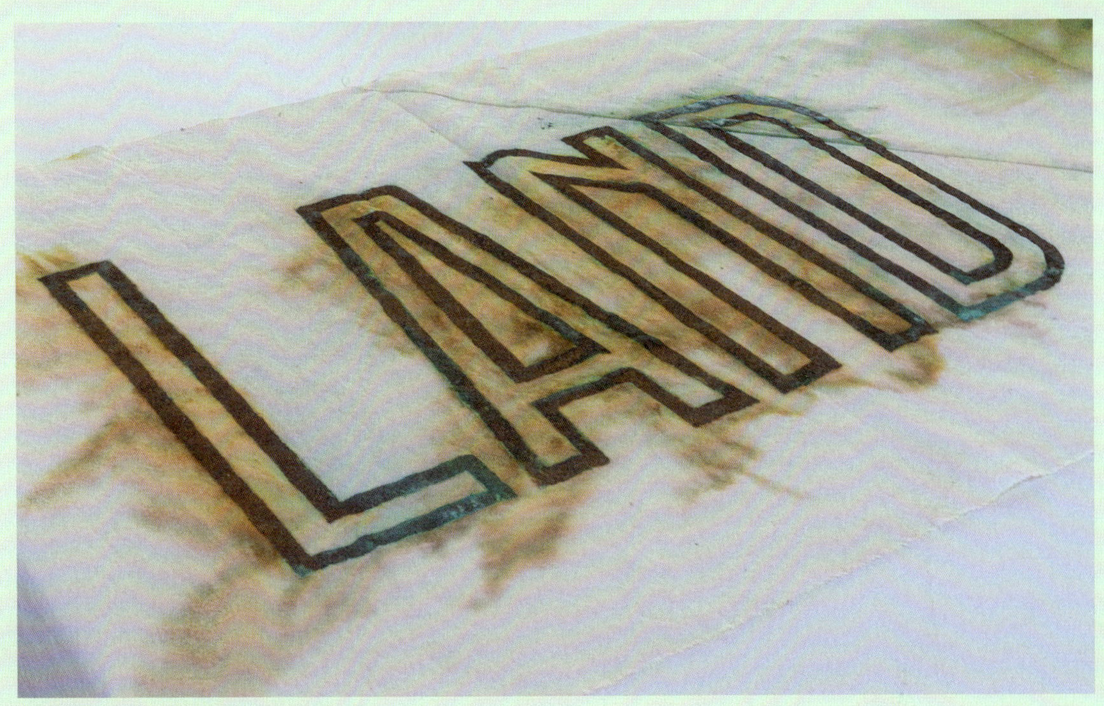

Detail of *To cut, to bleed, a rust-colored river*, 2024.

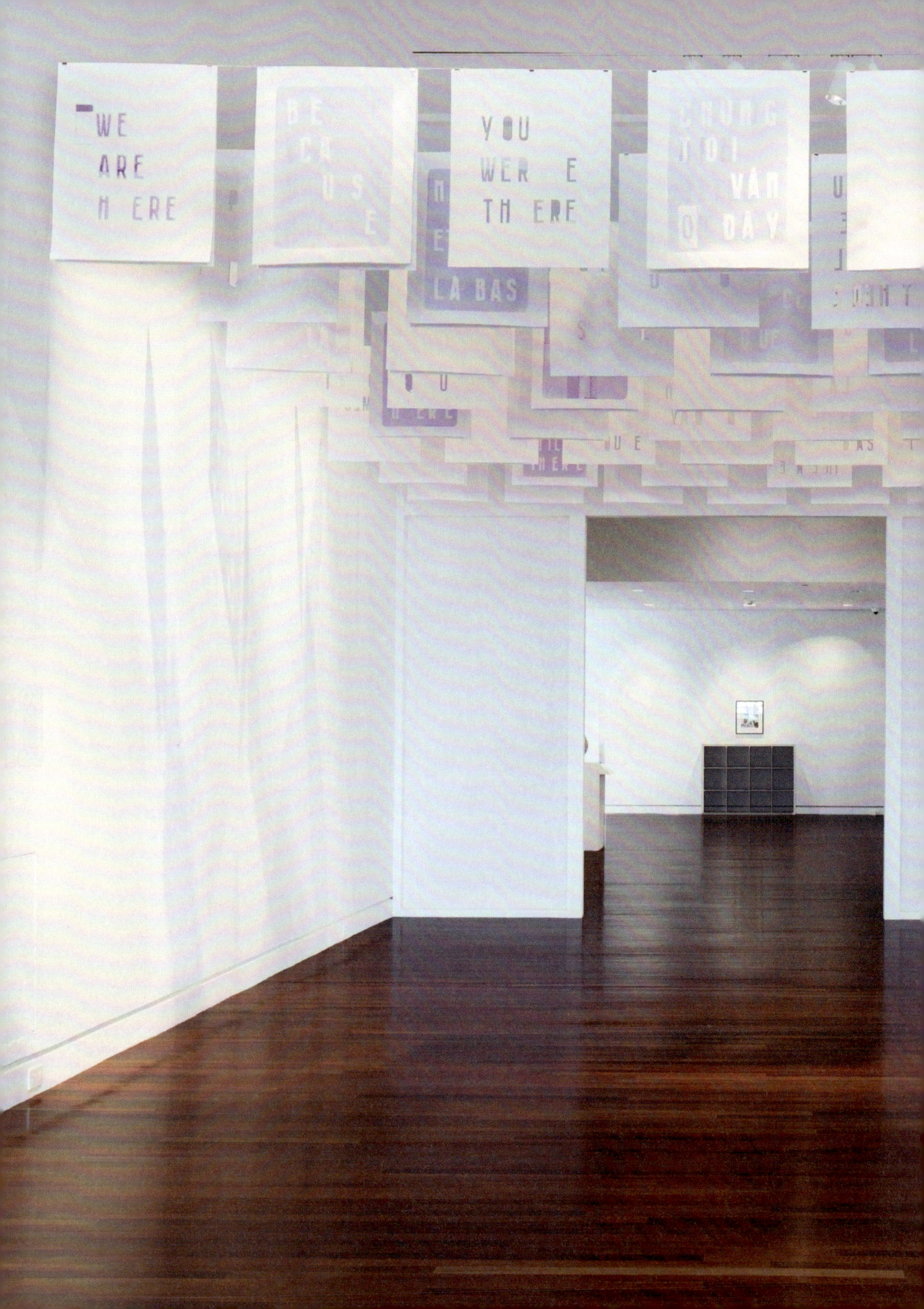
WE
ARE
YOU
LA BAS

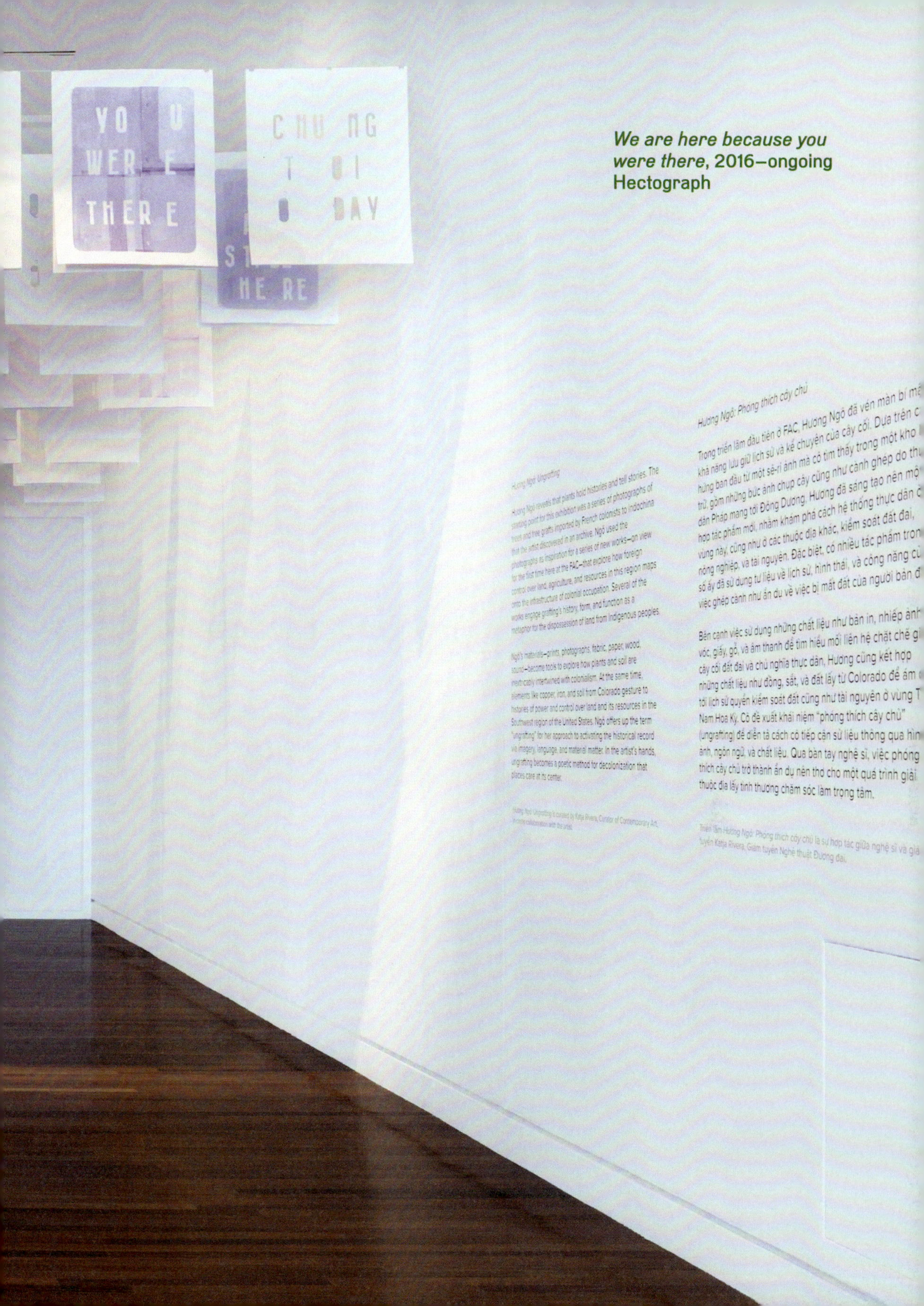

We are here because you were there, 2016–ongoing
Hectograph

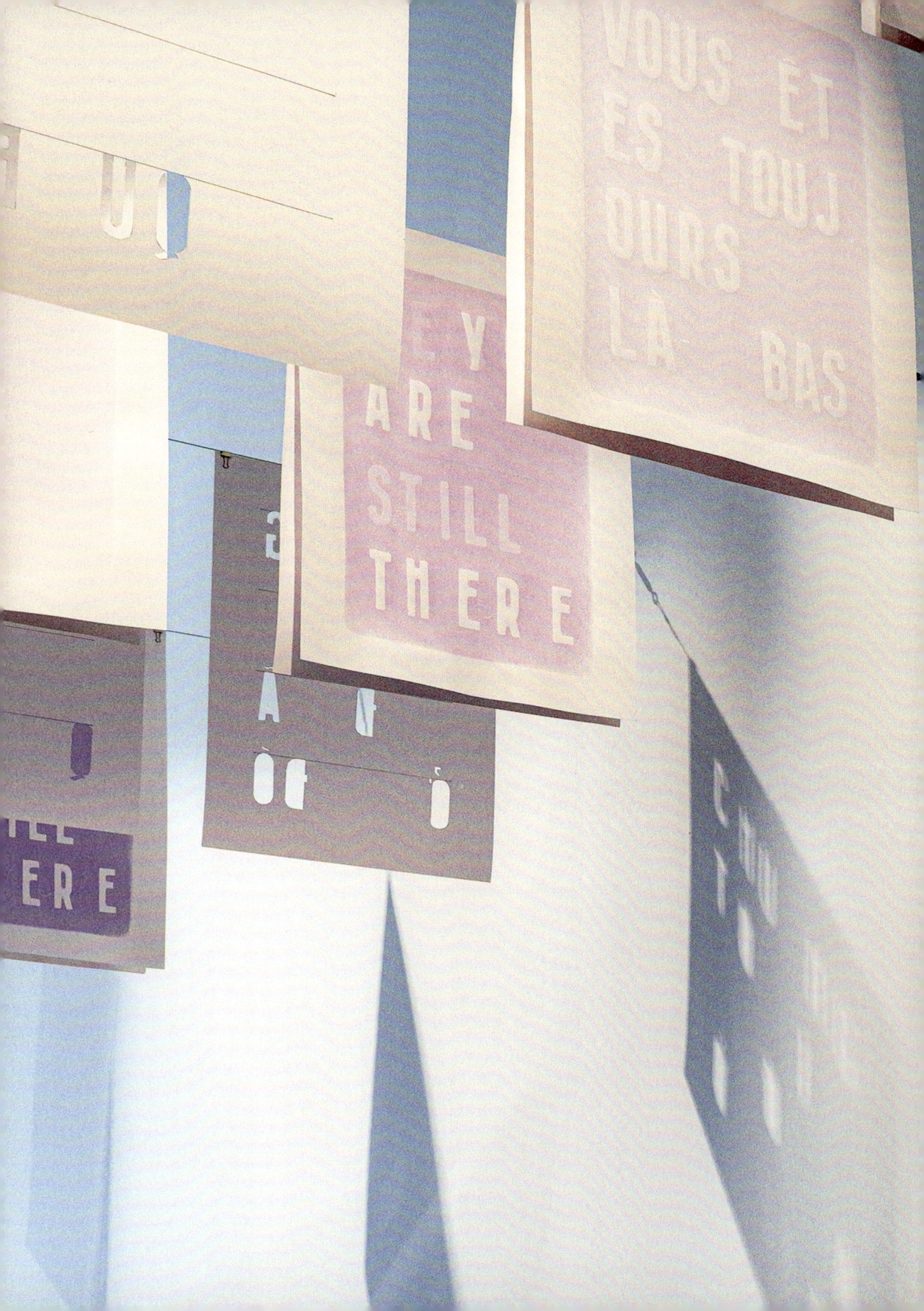
VOUS ET
ES TOUJ
OURS
LA BAS
ARE
STILL
THERE

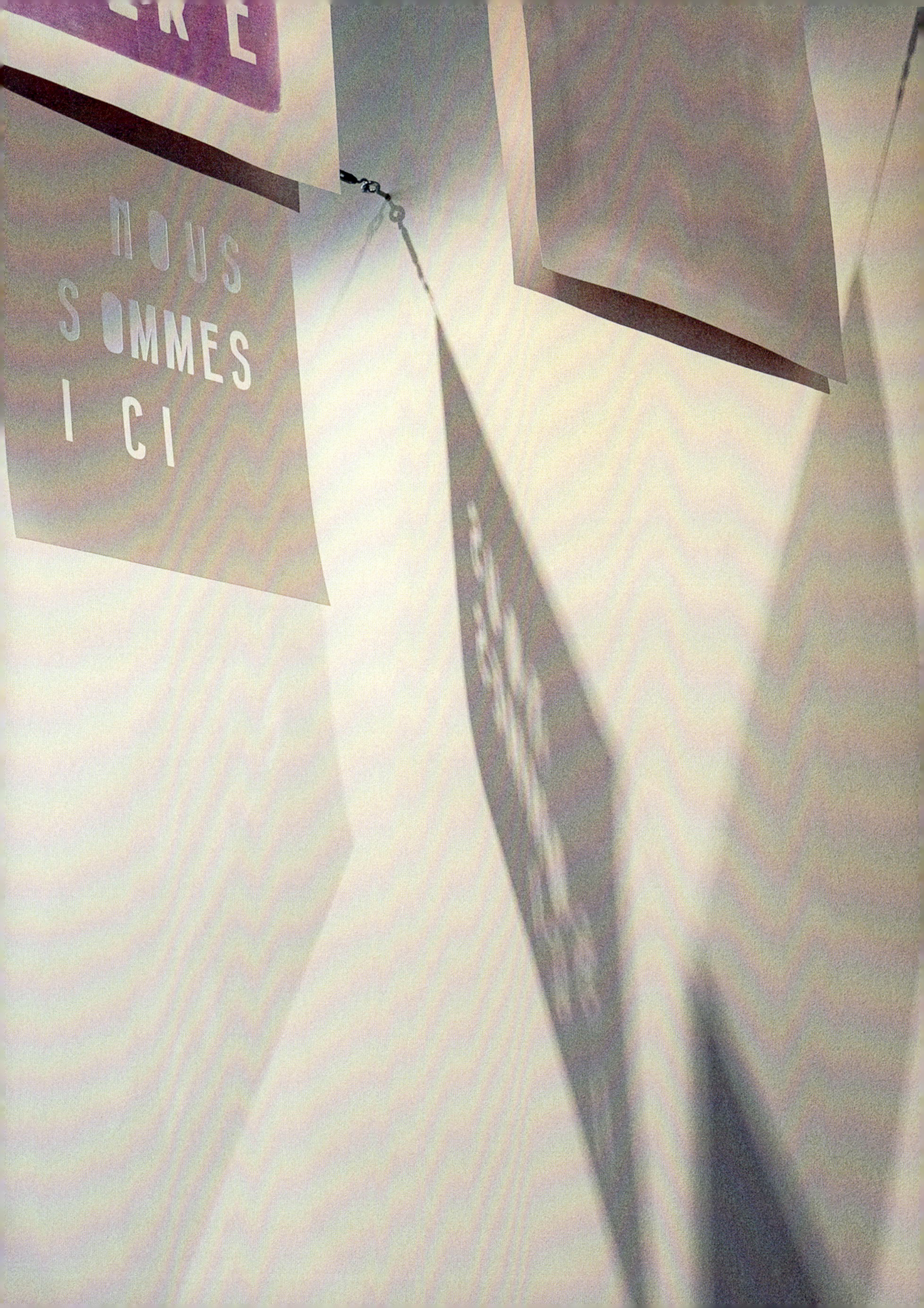
NOUS
SOMMES
ICI

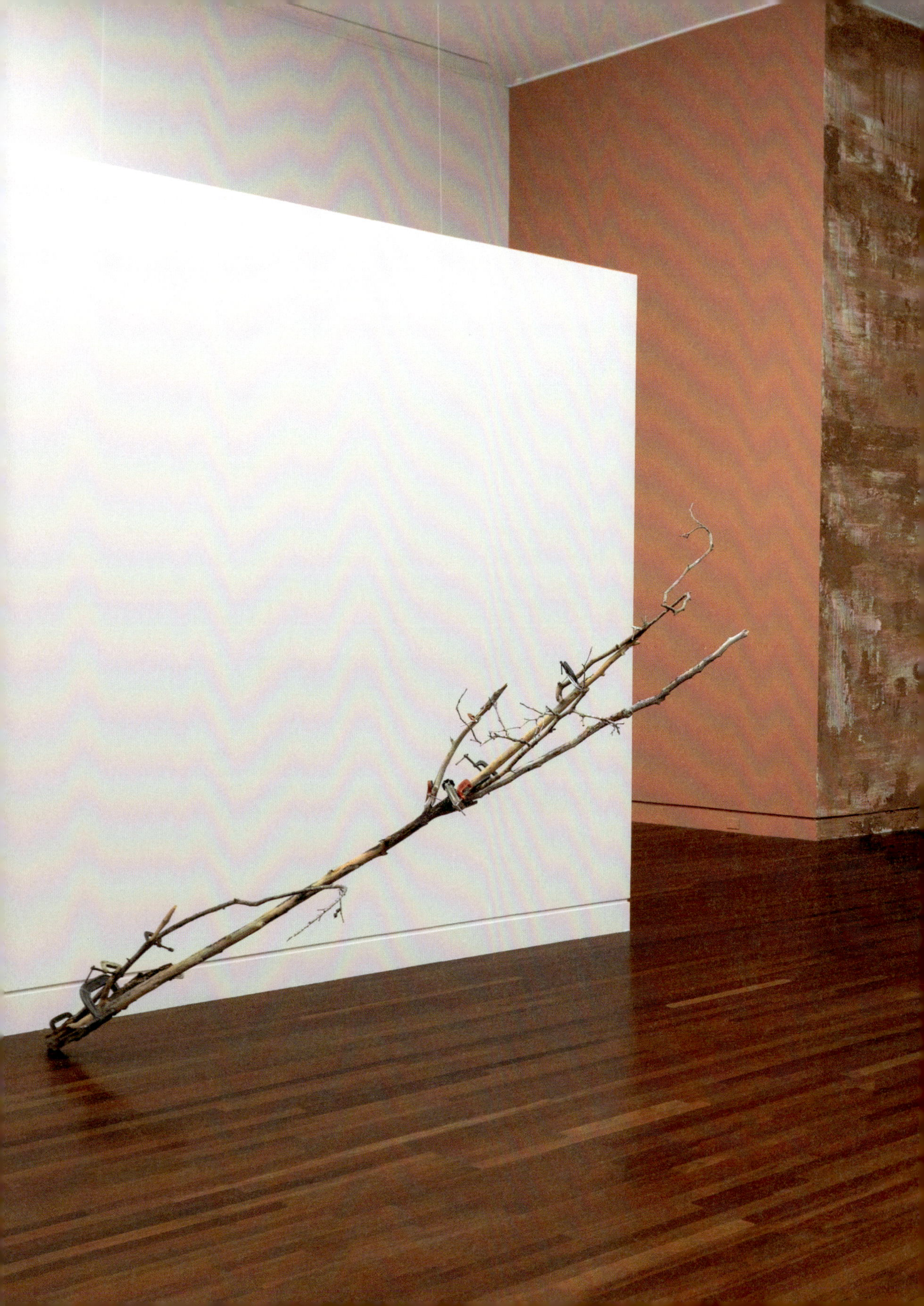

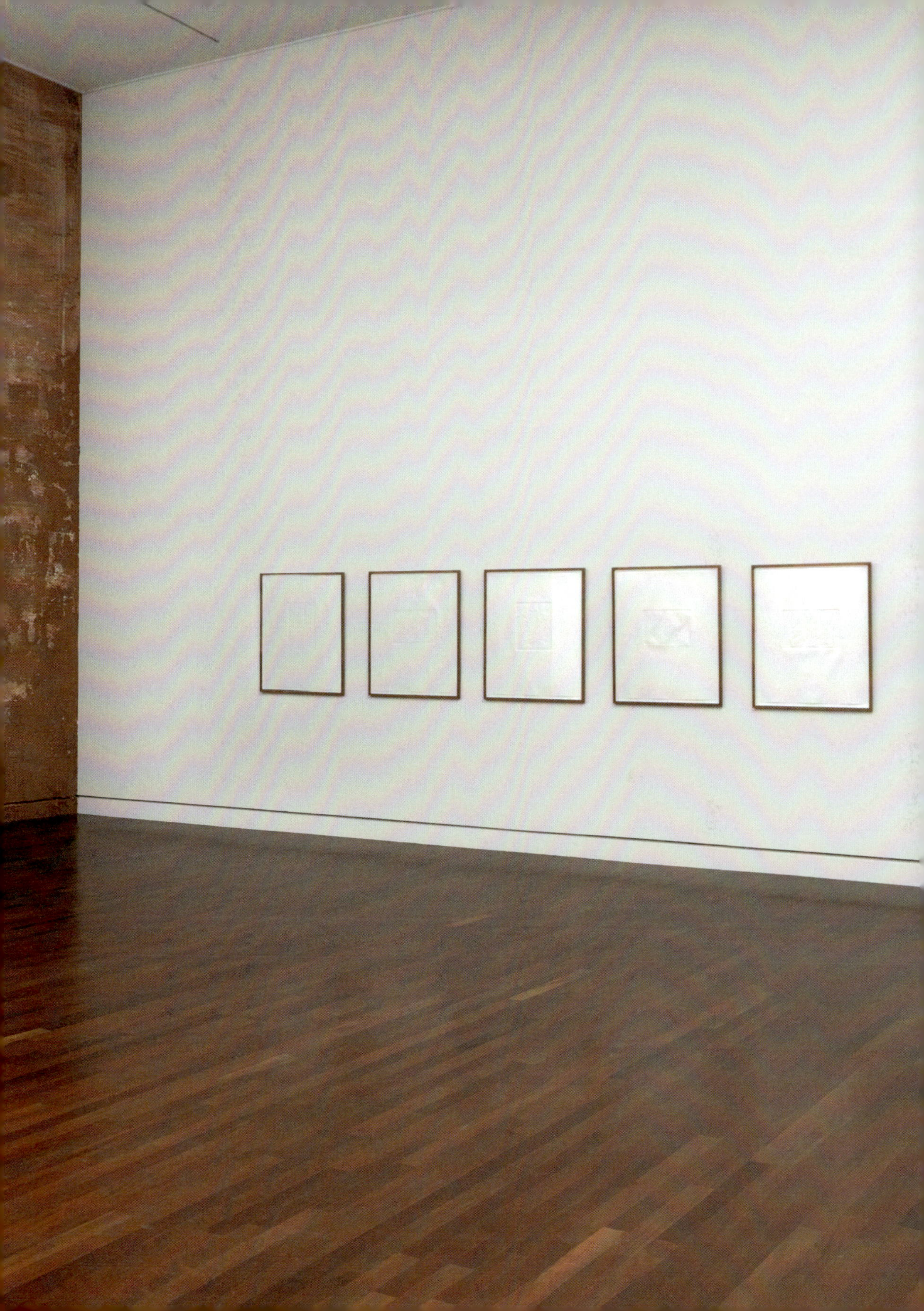

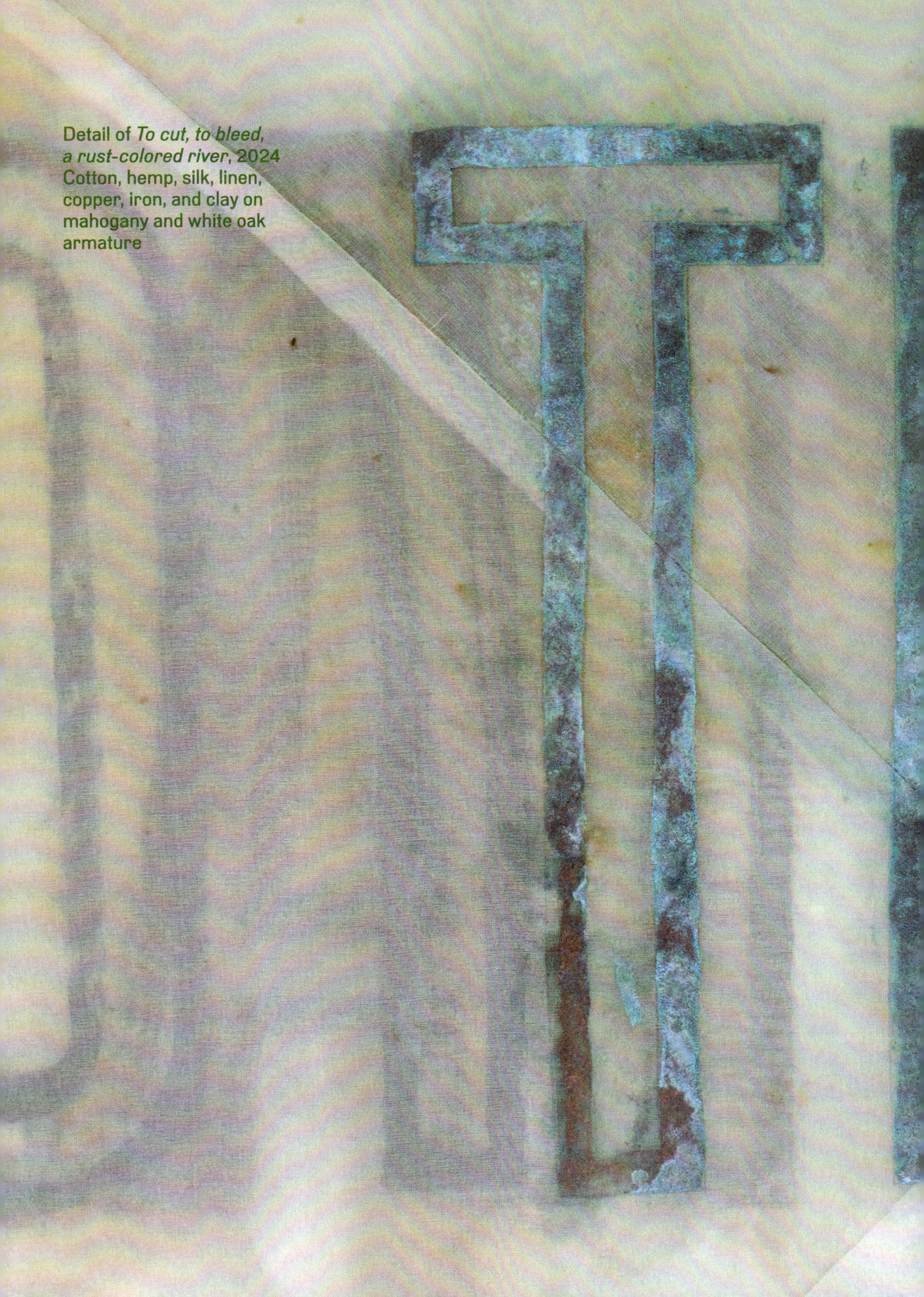

Detail of *To cut, to bleed, a rust-colored river*, 2024
Cotton, hemp, silk, linen, copper, iron, and clay on mahogany and white oak armature

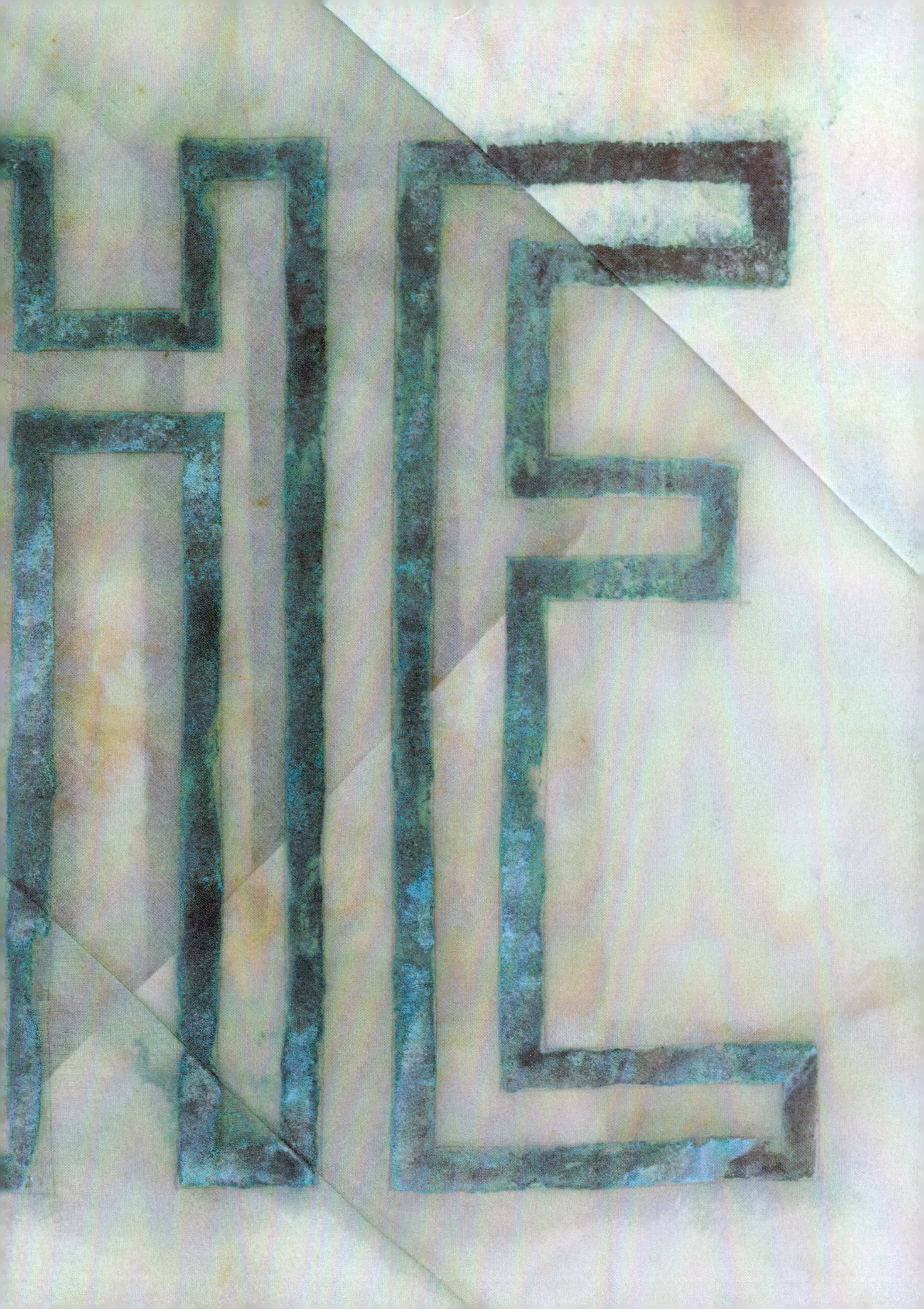

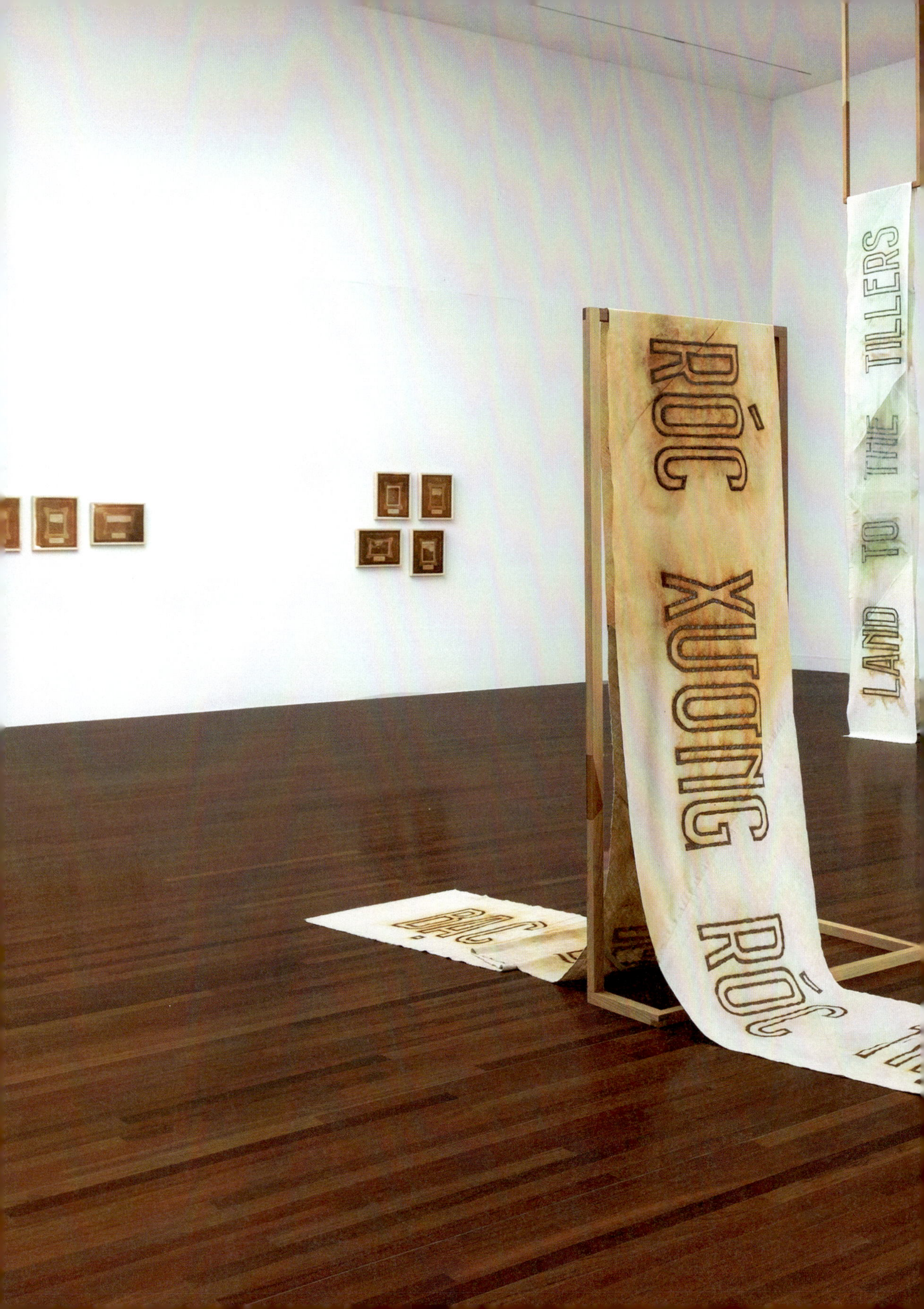
RÓC XƯƠNG
LAND TO THE TILLERS

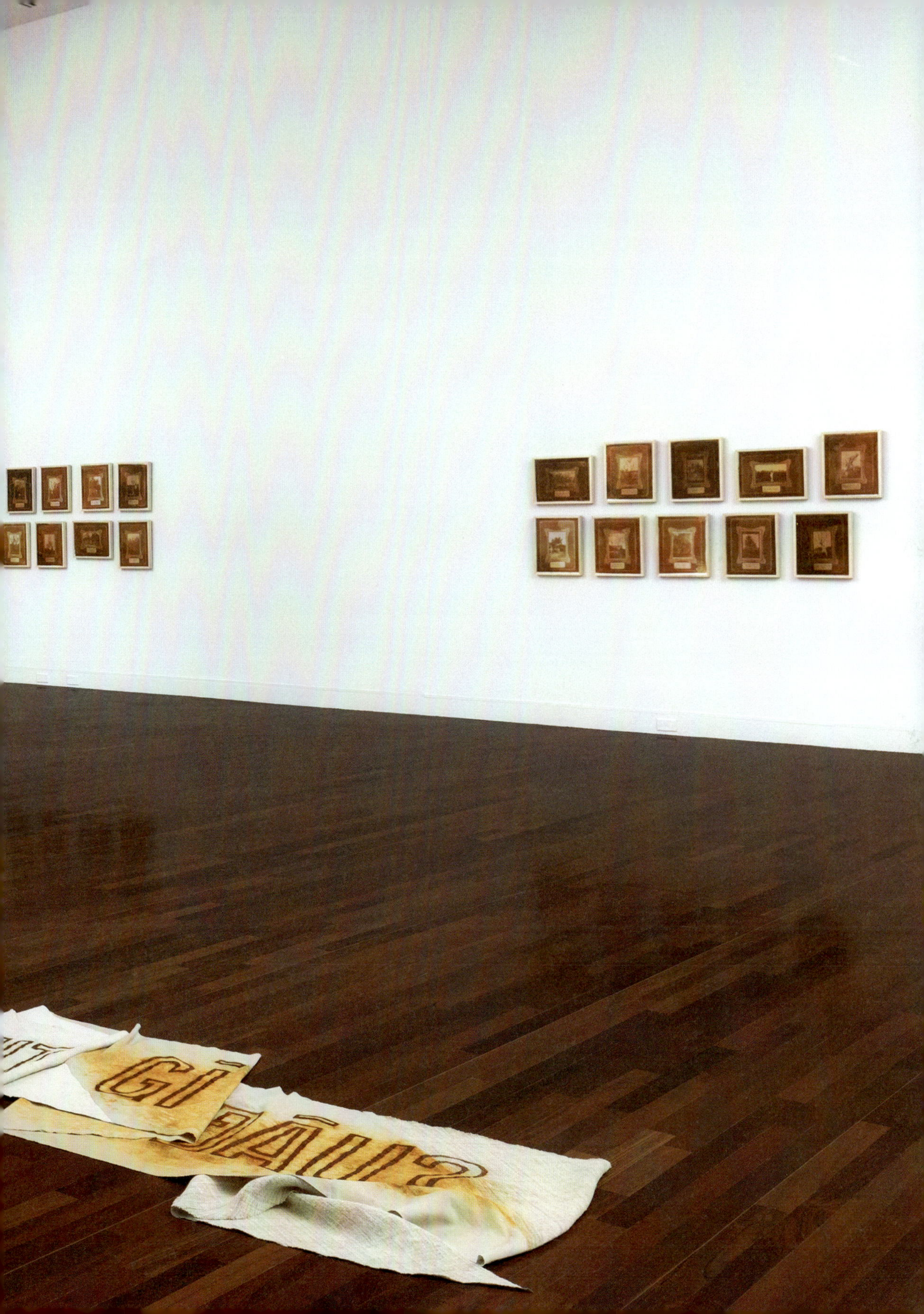

Latent Images (Grafts), 2024
Van Dyke prints on paper

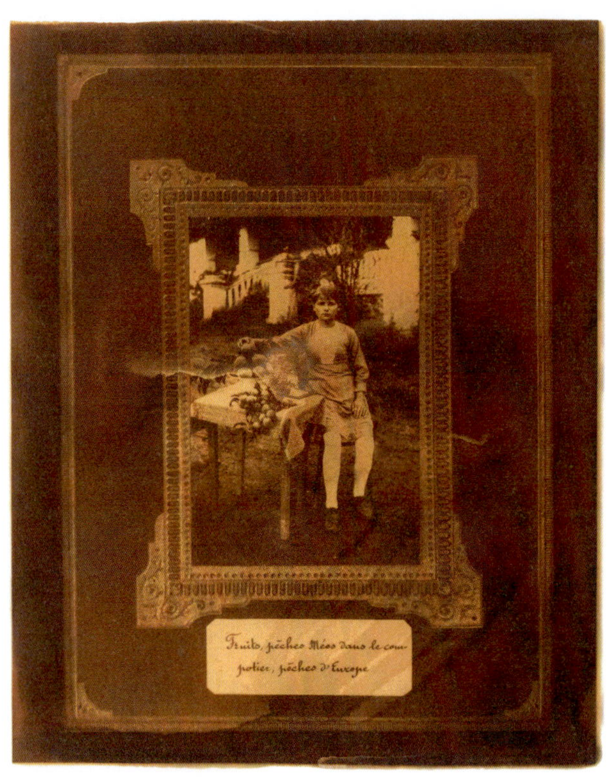

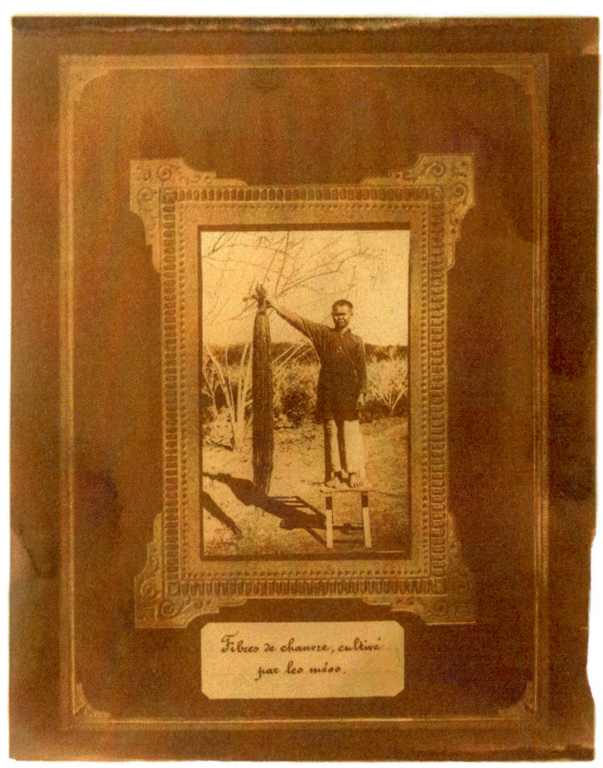

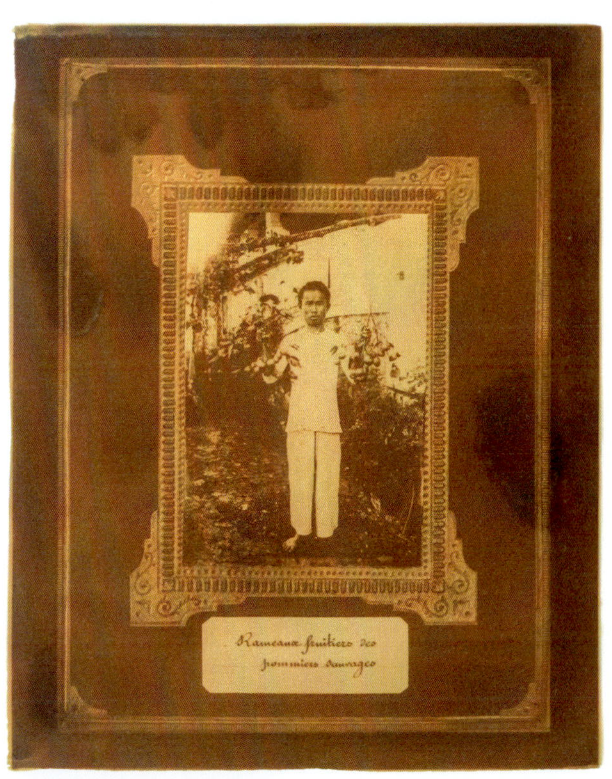
Rameaux fruitiers des
pommiers sauvages

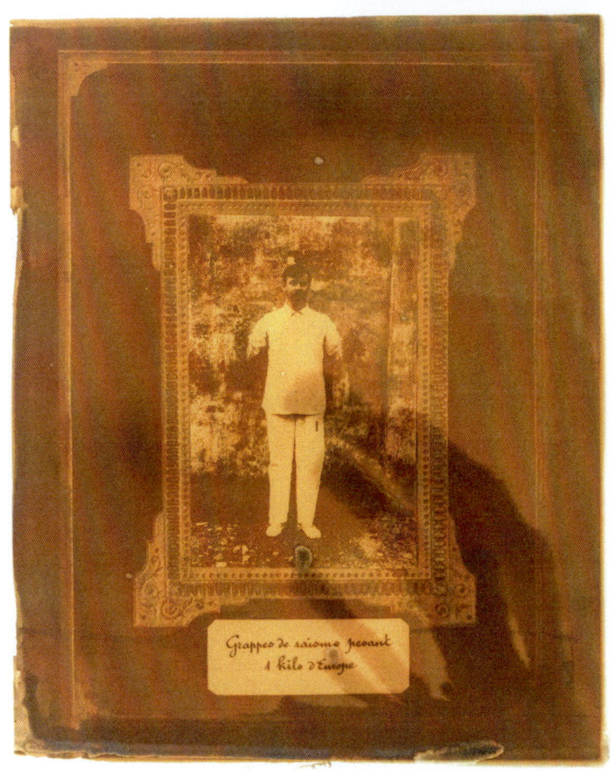
Grappes de raisins pesant
1 kilo d'Europe

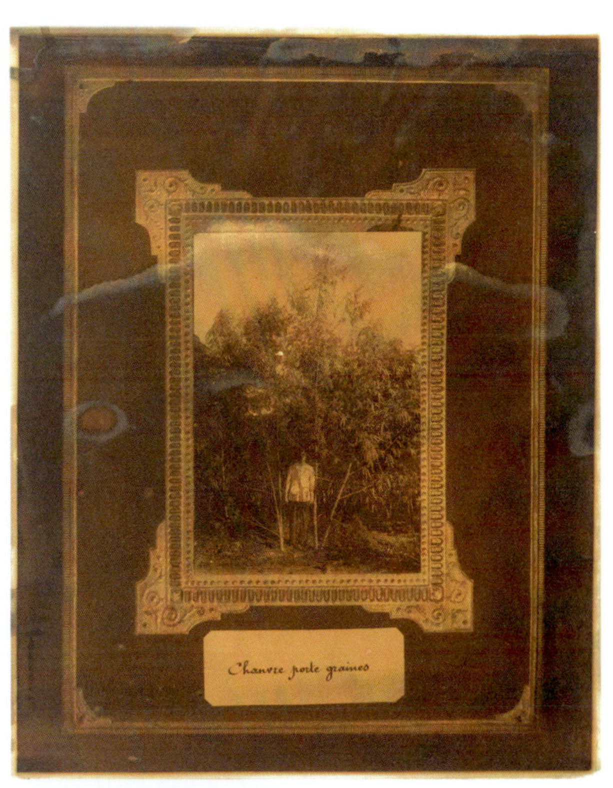
Chanvre porte graines

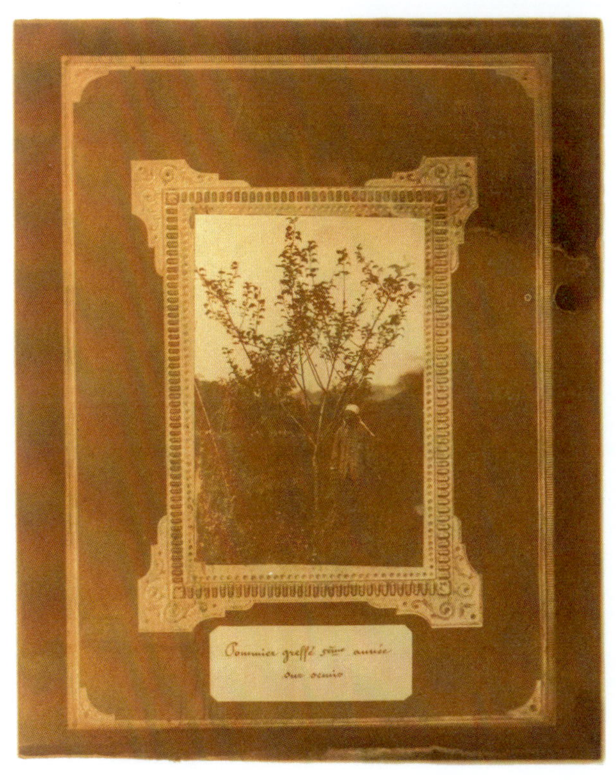
Pommier greffé 5ème année
du semis

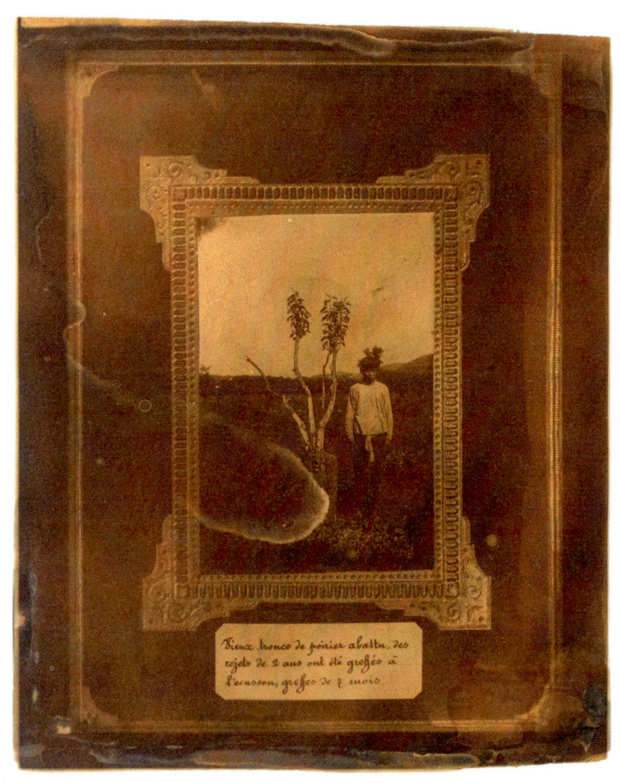
Vieux troncs de poirier abattu, des
rejets de 2 ans ont été greffés à
l'écusson, greffes de 7 mois.

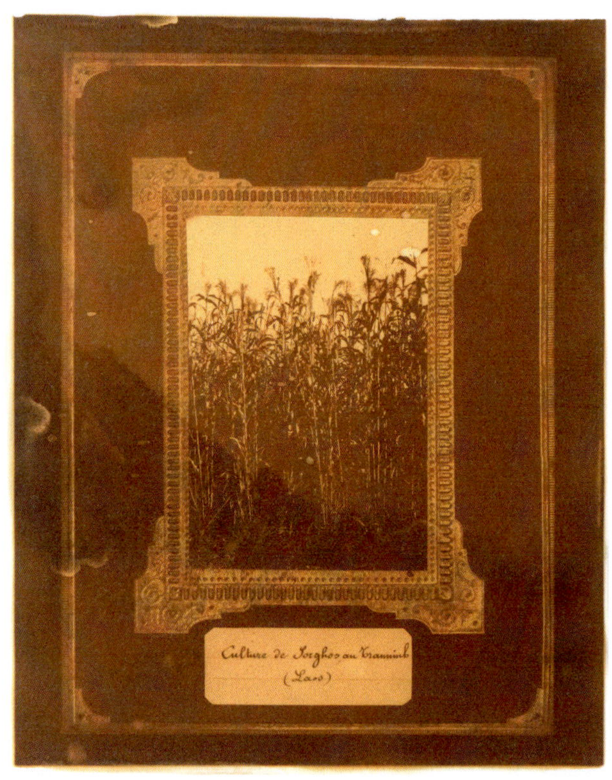
Culture de Sorghos au Tranninh
(Laos)

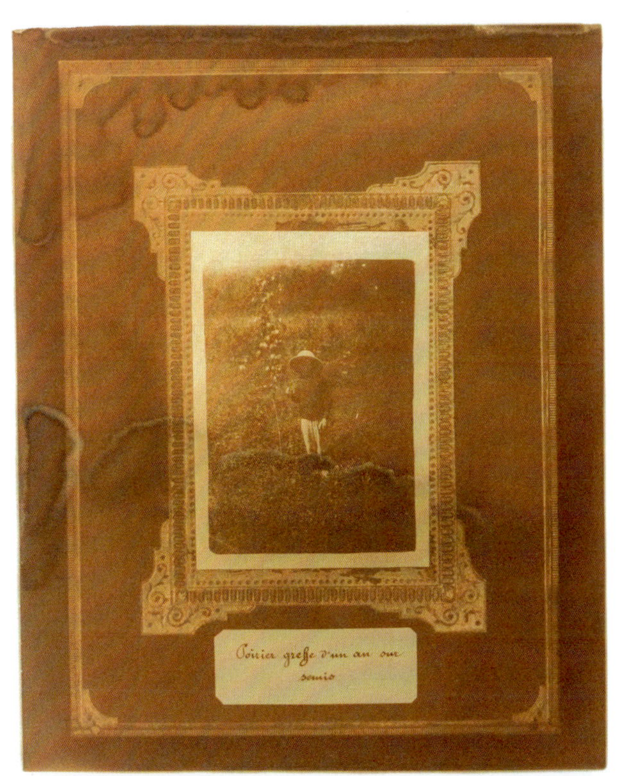
Poirier greffe d'un an sur
semis

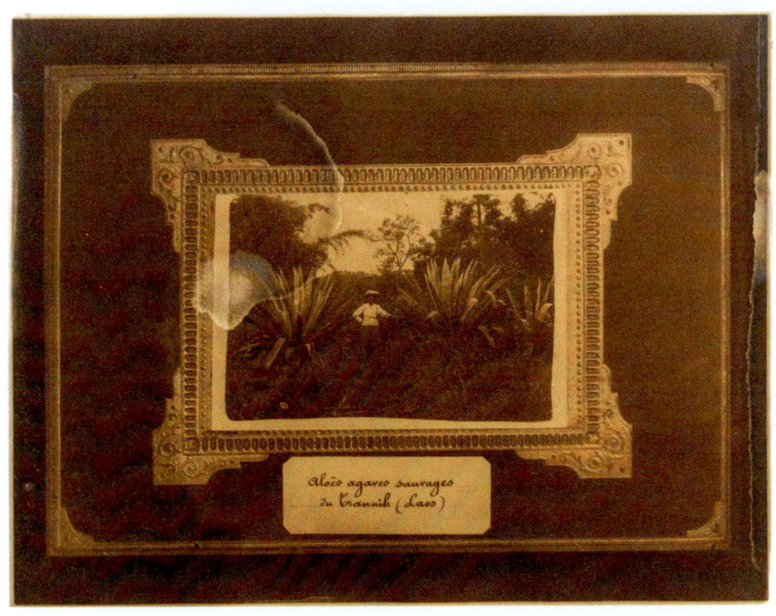
Aloès agaves sauvages
du Trannih (Laos)

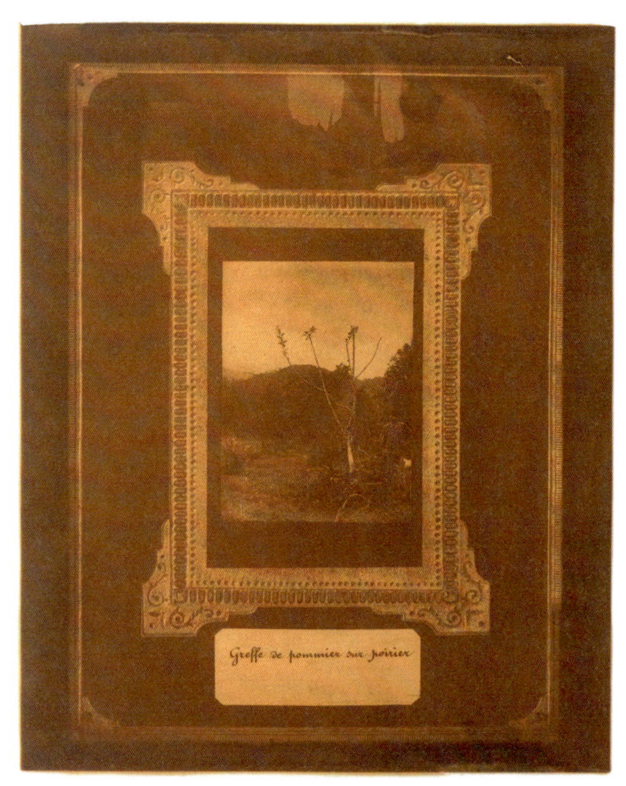
Greffe de pommier sur poirier

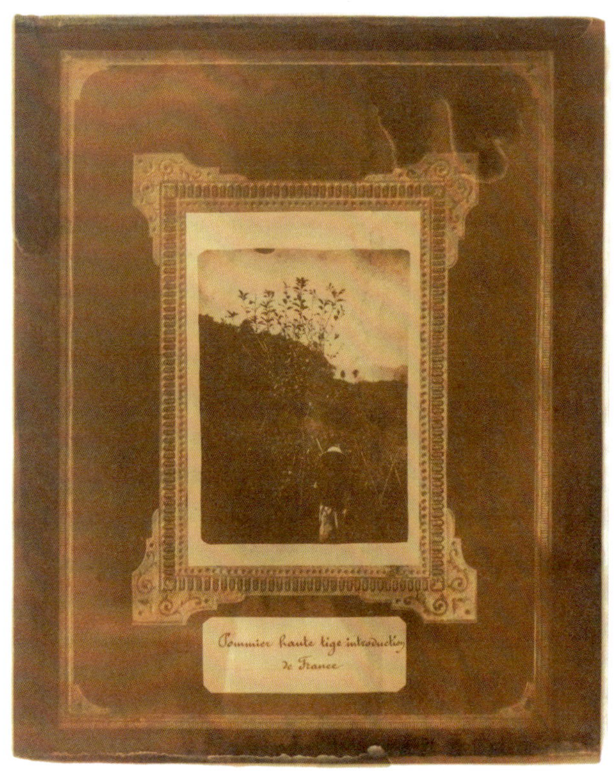
Pommier haute tige introduction
de France

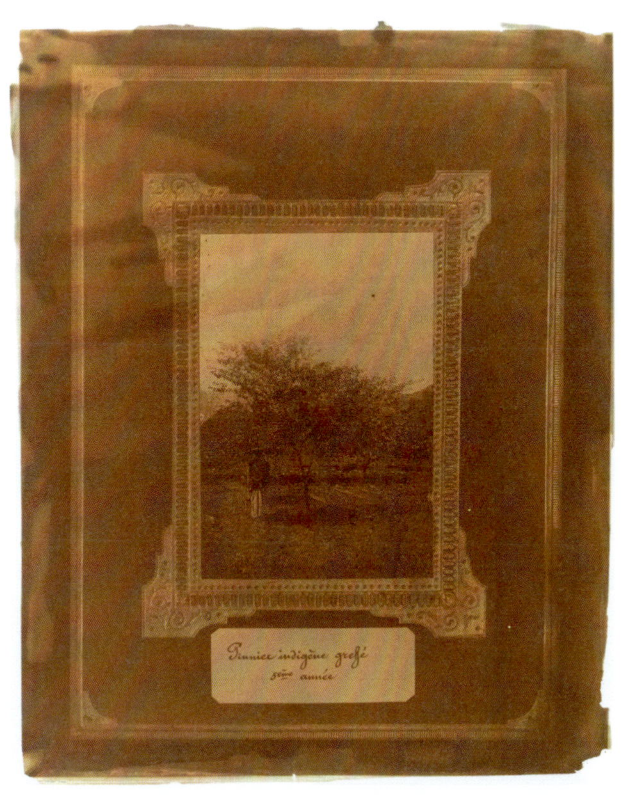
Prunier indigène greffé
5ème année

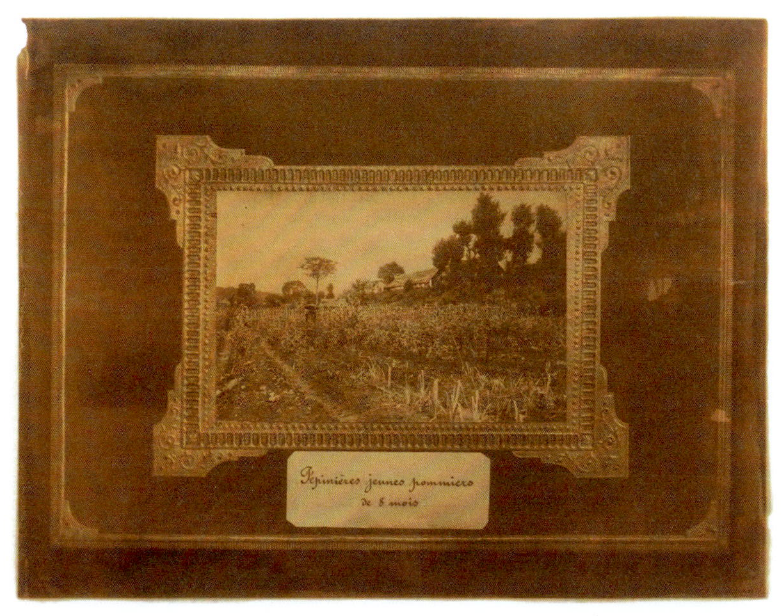
Pépinières jeunes pommiers
de 8 mois

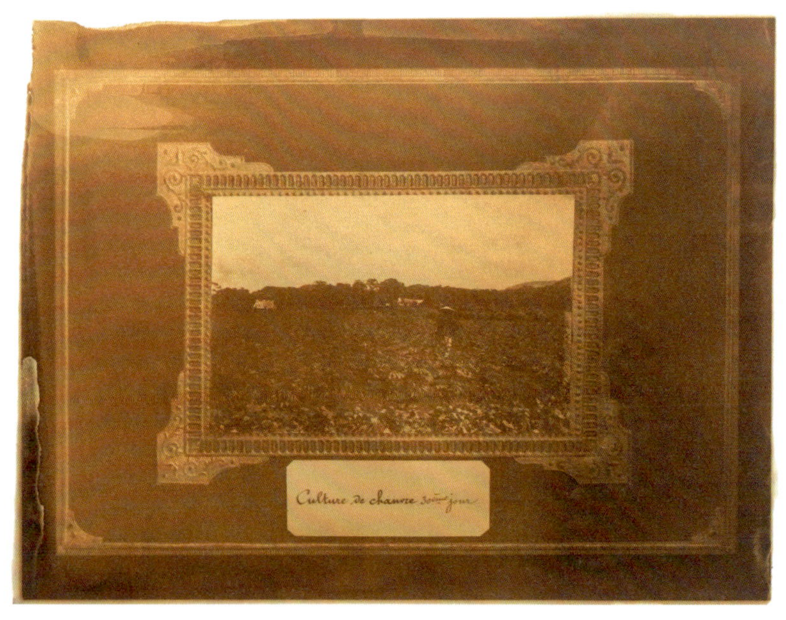
Culture de chanvre 30ème jour

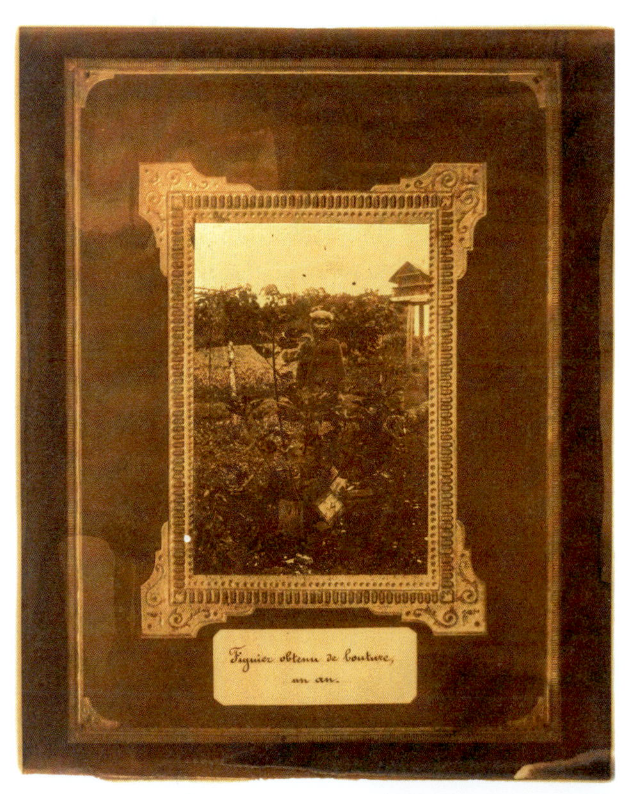
Figuier obtenu de bouture,
un an.

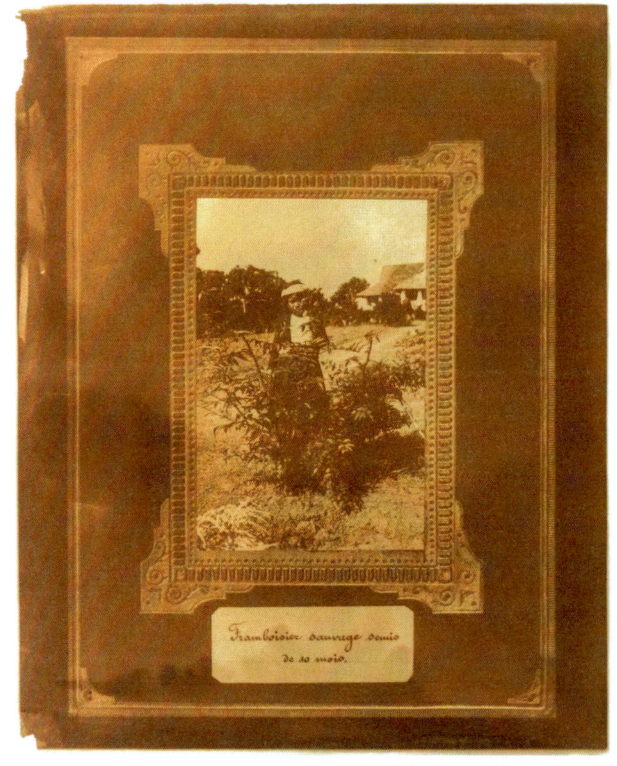
Framboisier sauvage semis
de 10 mois.

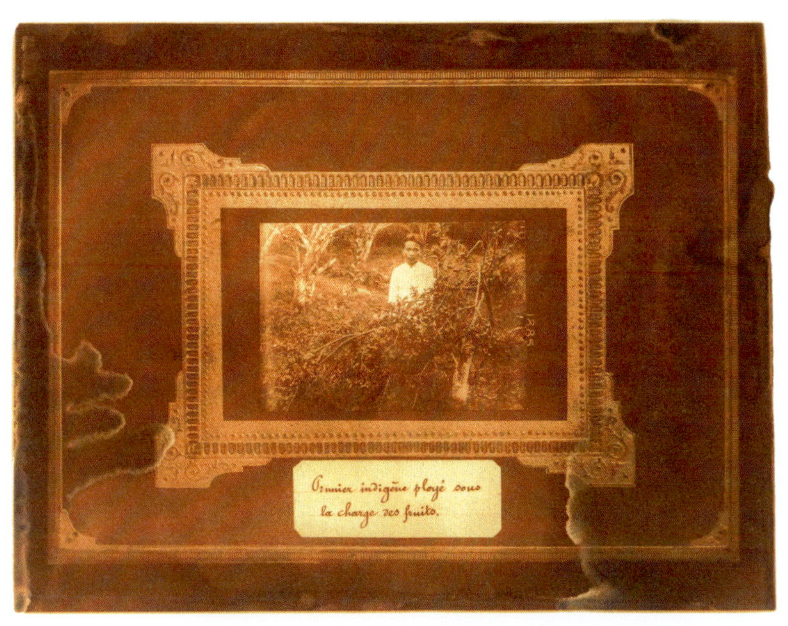
1885
Prunier indigène ployé sous
la charge des fruits.

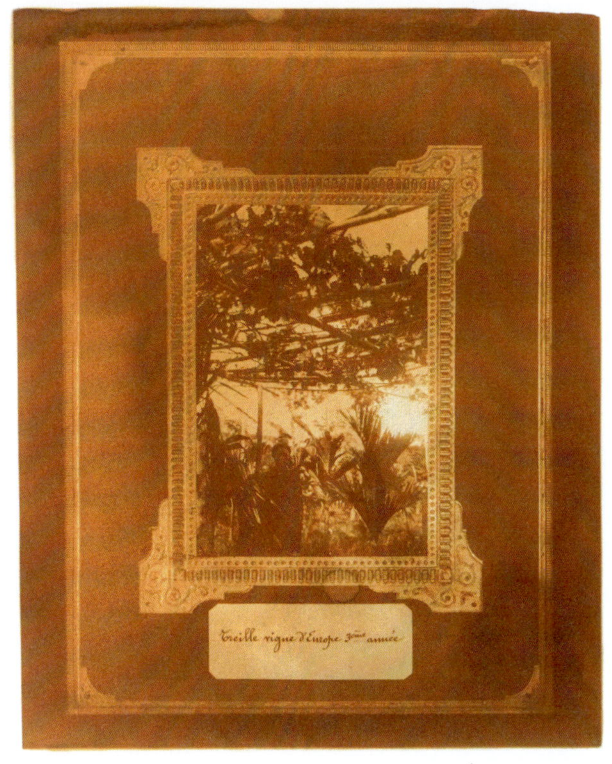
Treille vigne d'Europe 3ème année

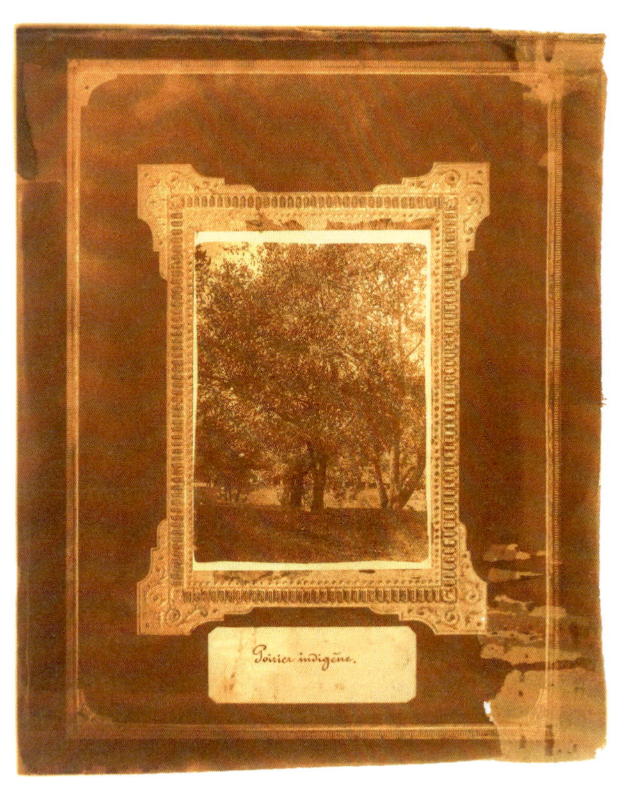
Poirier indigène.

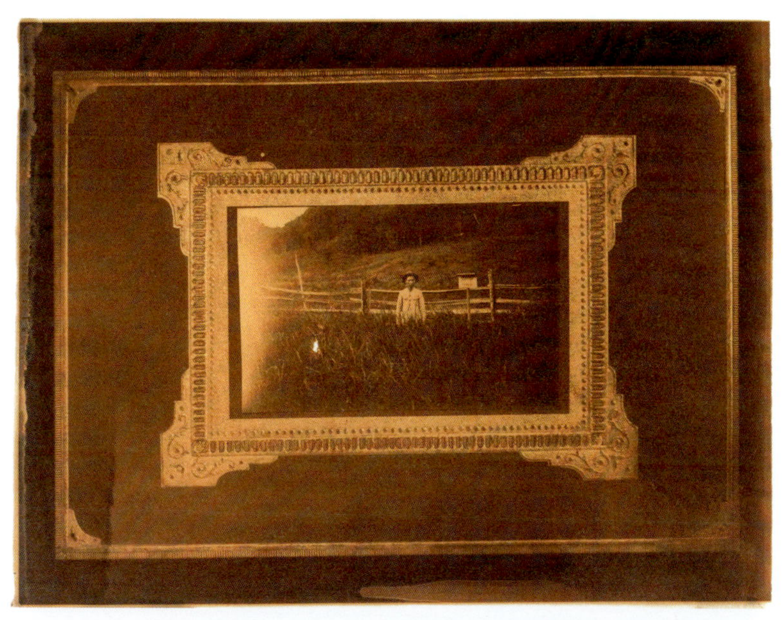

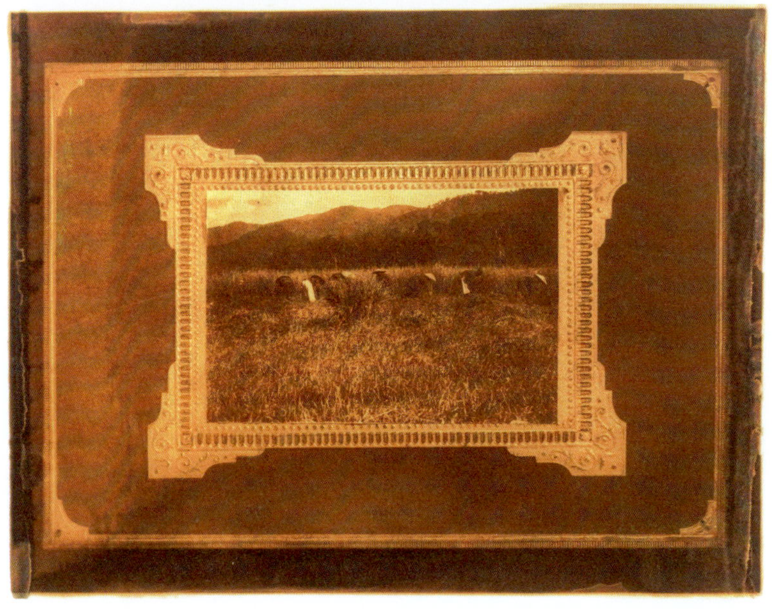

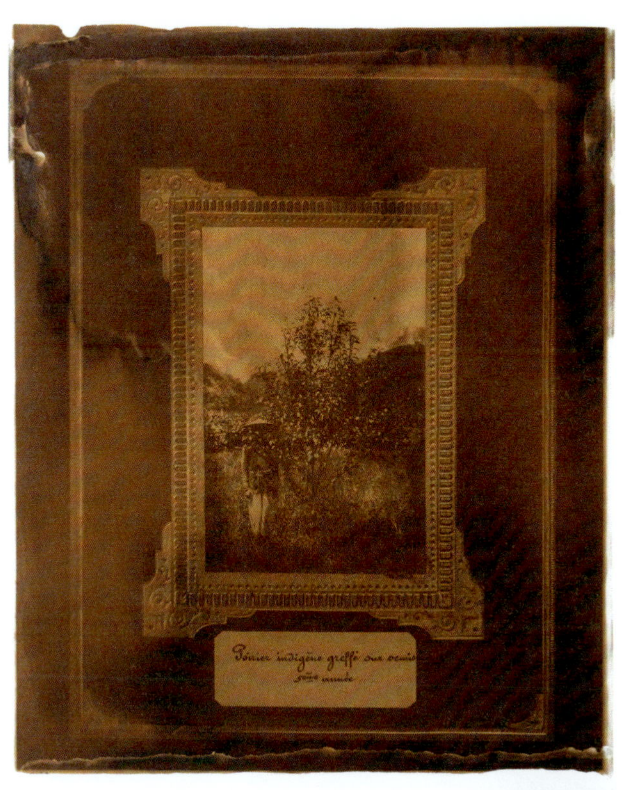
Poirier indigène greffé sur semis
5ème année

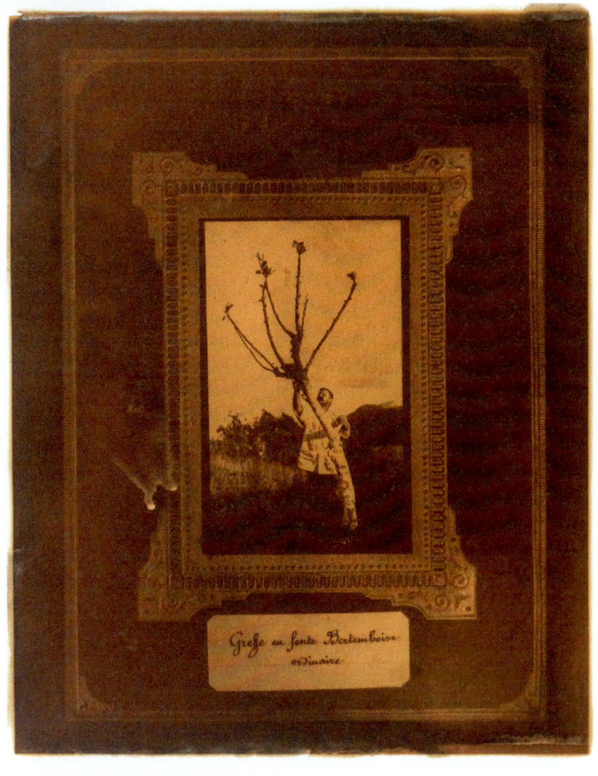
Greffe en fente Bertemboise
ordinaire

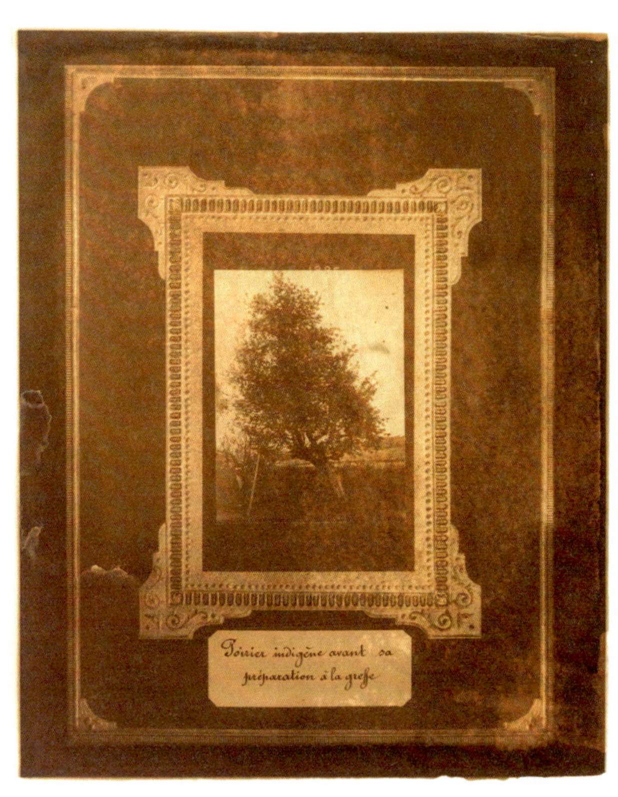
Poirier indigène avant sa
préparation à la greffe

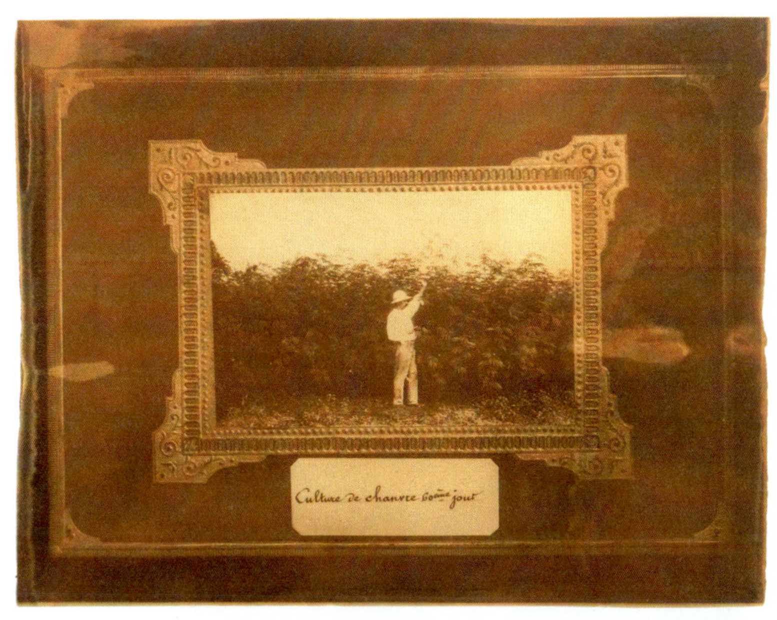
Culture de chanvre 60ème jour

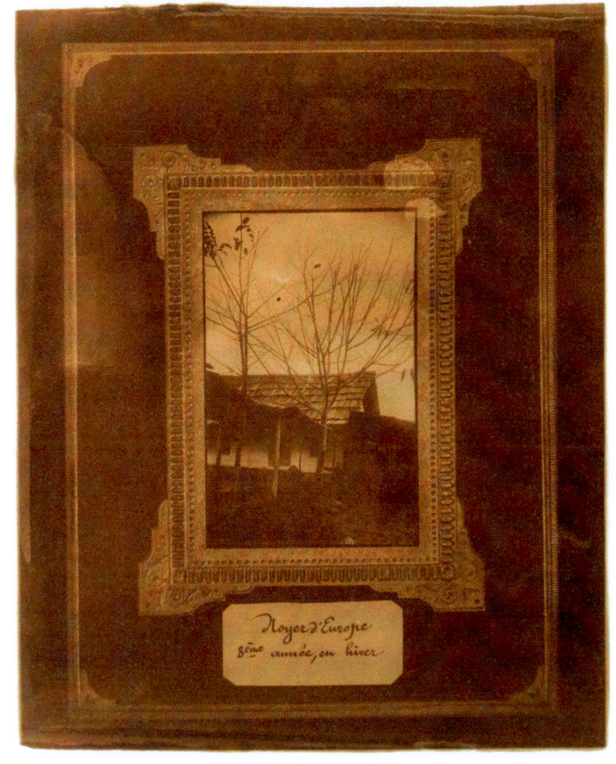
Noyer d'Europe
8ème année, en hiver

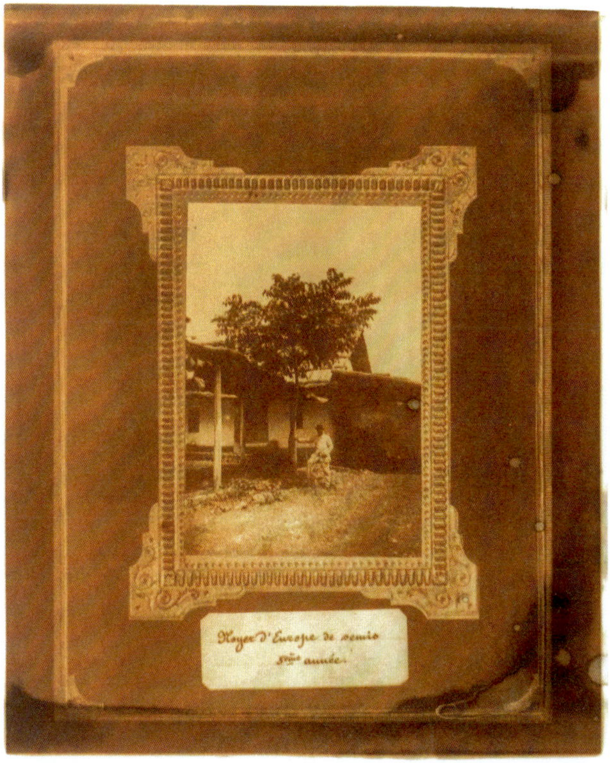
Foyer d'Europe de Semio
3ème année.

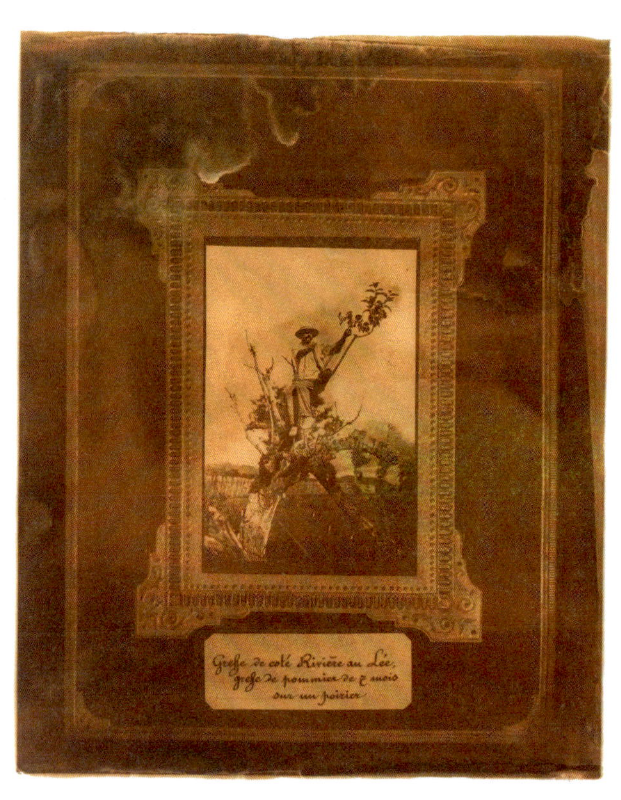
Greffe de coté Rivière au Lée,
greffe de pommier de 7 mois
sur un poirier

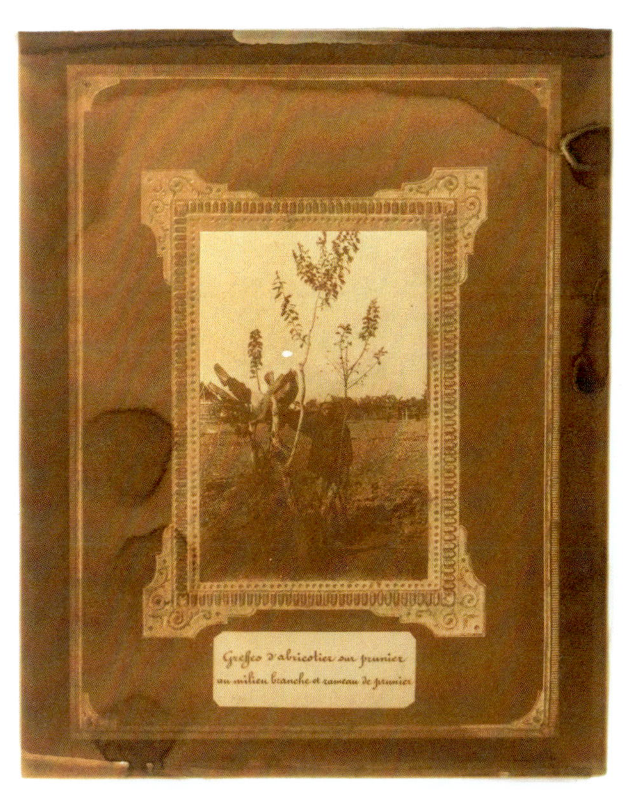
Greffes d'abricotier sur prunier
au milieu branche et rameau de prunier

A POETICS OF THE GRAFT: LISTENING FOR CARE IN HƯƠNG NGÔ'S UNGRAFTING

JUSTIN QUANG NGUYÊN PHAN

A close engagement with the archive—its status, form, and function—reverberates through Hương Ngô's broader artistic oeuvre. Contemplating the techniques and materials that structure personal and institutional archives straddling France and Vietnam, Ngô has tracked the enduring significance of the French Empire and its visual regime. In exhibitions like *To Name It Is To See It* (2017) and *It Was Her Handwriting That Gave Her Away* (2020), which partially follows how Vietnamese revolutionary figure Nguyễn Thị Minh Khai eluded French surveillance technologies by manipulating her visual appearance and writing manifestos, Ngô presents a coeval dynamic: the continuous articulation of Vietnamese women's anticolonial nationalism and intersectional Marxism/anti-Fascism despite, and at times precisely because of, French counterinsurgency during the early twentieth century.

Ngo's *Ungrafting* (2024) builds on these previous works and carefully reminds us of the synchronous reality between French colonial imaginaries and the visually indexed lives of the colonized. The root of the exhibition is the work of René Tétard, a government-employed photographer for Governor General of French Indochina Albert Sarraut, who took forty-nine photographs in 1919 in and around an orchard or farm in Indochina. These photographs made their way into a collection now housed in Les Archives nationales d'outre mer (the archives of overseas territories) in France. Almost a century later, Ngô came across this collection in her own research into French attempts to surveil and suppress twentieth-century Vietnamese revolutionaries. Inspired by these photographs, Ngô's *Ungrafting* reproduces the photographs as a series of thirty-eight Van Dyke prints titled *Latent Images (Grafts)*. Featuring trees and plants, Ngô's rendition of the photographs reveals a selectively unacknowledged presence: racialized peoples—whether Kinh, Hmong, French—placed beside the plants for scale.

Engaging her own background in biology, *Ungrafting* emerges within Ngô's contentions with science as a project of military and imperial knowledge to suggest a poetics of the graft. Grafting can be commonly understood as the scientific or agricultural process of binding two plants. Yet, as *Latent Images (Grafts)* might demonstrate, French aims to graft fruits and trees in Vietnam's landscape are moored by colonial agriculture and racist pseudo-science within the French civilizing mission. In a recent presentation, Ngô examines photographs taken during Tétard's decade-long tenure working with Sarraut and how the scientific domestication of plants also functions as a metaphor that manifested across colonial genres, speaking visually to the placatability of once threatening ethnic minority groups to French colonization.

Collectively, then, *Ungrafting* indexes images of French colonialism that demand us to complicate an ocular-centric way of seeing and urges us instead to *listen*. Can you perceive the image's collective and individual sound? In listening, what forms of presence and absence do we sense? In her own study of photographs, Black feminist and visual studies scholar Tina Campt calls on us to notice how images function sonically across a mix of higher and lower frequencies. Building on Campt's provocation, Ngô's work gestures to a methodology of care that doesn't wholly reproduce the visual archive of French colonialism. She names ungrafting to describe how she "activat[es] the historical record via imagery, language, and material matter. In her hands, ungrafting becomes a poetic method for decolonization that places care [at] its center." We can read Ngô's method as a means of listening for and enacting care by intimating incommensurable historical moments. In so doing, she lets us hear the poetics across art, science, history, and geography to see how care is afforded, acknowledged, and absented across these various genres.

Listening to care in the exhibition's other pieces allows us to see how Ngô reconfigures the connections drawn between human and nonhuman life. On one end, we have *Studies for Translation* (2024). Here, she installs photographs of herbarium samples collected from the French colonies for the Muséum national d'Histoire naturelle in Paris alongside living plants that could have equally been taken from these same colonies. On the other end, we have *Da/Skin (I, II)*, a gestural play on texture and textile as Ngô creates skin/fake paper grafts that are then hand-stitched together. Taken together, we can consider how knowledge about plants, paper, and skin produced during this period relied upon scientific design to accumulate resources, analyze specimens, and administer a vision of agriculture that would purportedly create "value" for the economic demands of colonial racial capitalism.

Such poetic resonances in human/nonhuman life within *Ungrafting* are also explored in parts of the exhibition that traveled through and connected seemingly disparate geographies. Before it came to Colorado, the first iteration of *Latent Images (Grafts)* was presented in New Orleans as part of the exhibition *Cuộc bể dâu/The sea turns into mulberry fields and the mulberry field turns into the sea* (2021), in which Ngô explored French colonial failures in establishing silk trade in Vietnam and Louisiana in order to situate French colonialism's resonance across its overseas territories past and present. Here, how we imagine the geo-graph, a writing of the earth via inter-imperial plantation economies and capital accumulation, is revealed to be wrapped up in the material and symbolic poetics of grafts. *Latent Images*' site-specificity in Colorado Springs brings together seemingly ungrafted regions—Southeast Asia, the American South, and the American Southwest—and beckons our own reckoning with the intimacies of French and Spanish colonization in the Americas.

Moreover, by focusing on how her artistic manipulation evokes care, we can sense how Ngô's handling of medium also engenders possibilities for both ruination and repair. In reprinting Tétard's photographs, Ngô chooses—in *Latent Images (Grafts)*—to alter the printing process. By "unfixing" the Van Dyke prints, Ngô activates a dormant force within the photograph and lets them deteriorate and darken over time, transforming the life of the archival document in the process. Ngô's gesture points to the paradoxical need to fix by unfixing; thus, unfixing is simultaneously and nonsensically an attempt of ruinous, reparative care.

Similar to how *Studies for Ungrafting* (2024) uses blind-embossed printing to print without ink, *Latent Images (Grafts)* plays with form to create another image by trusting what autonomously forms from what lies beneath. In this way, Ngô's exhibition models the significance of care in the histories and genealogies we draw; how we enunciate the colonial, anticolonial, and decolonial boundaries of art, science, history, and geography; and ultimately how we imagine a future for whose terms are not fixed, captured, and predetermined by capital, race, and empire but instead attuned to a lifegiving force from below.

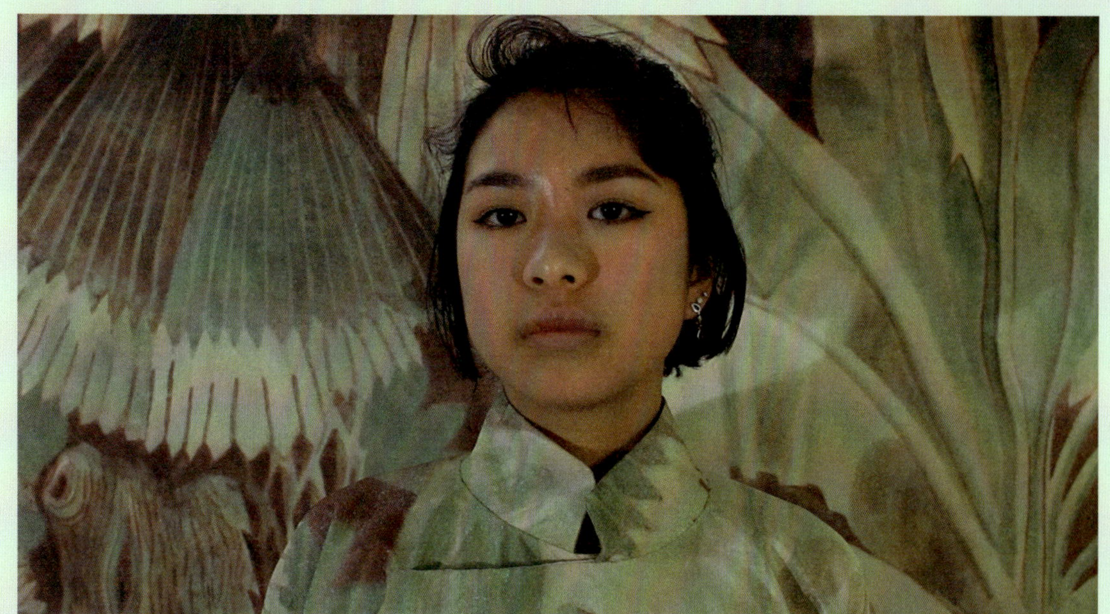

Still from *Having Been Lost in Plain View*, 2017.

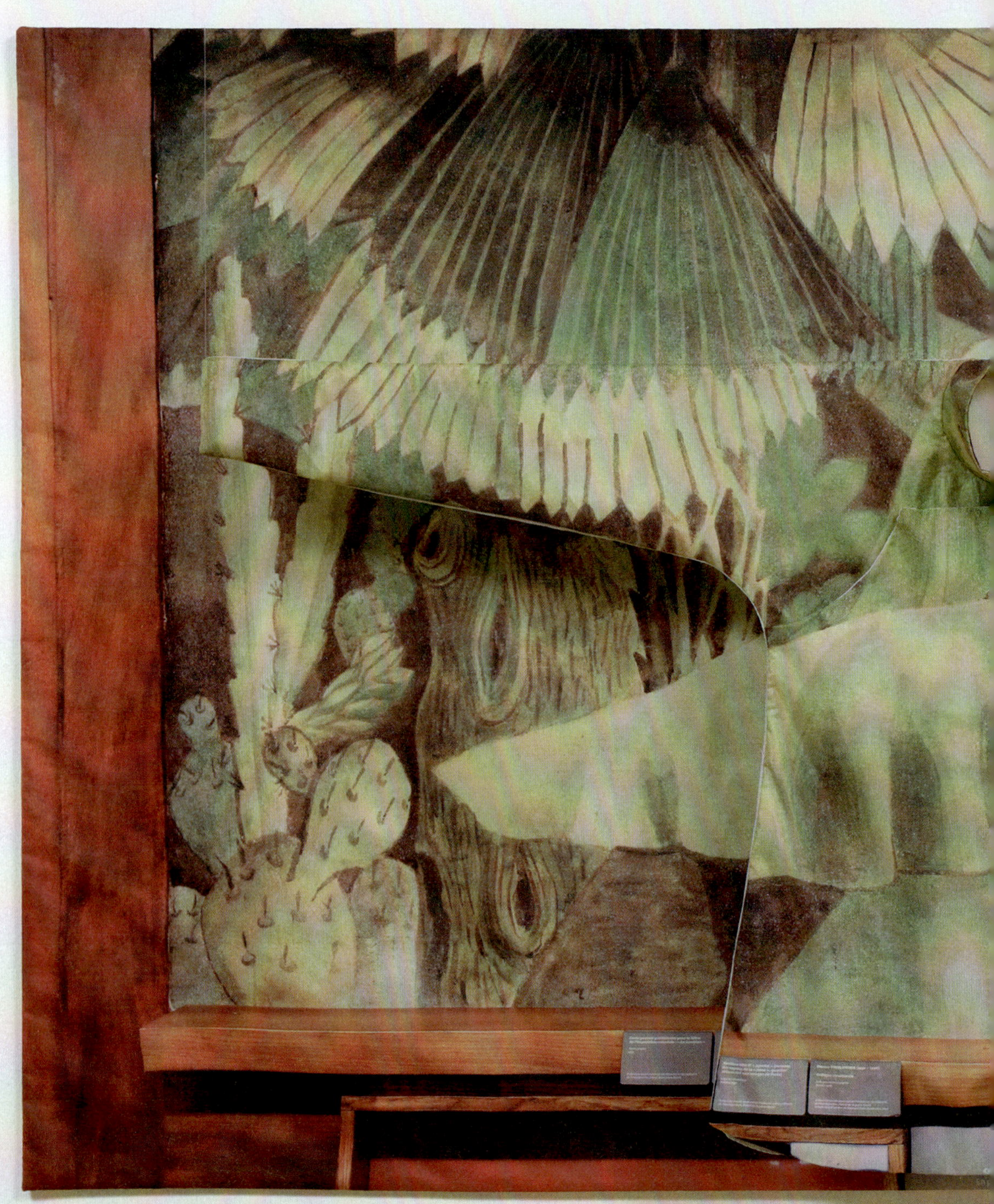

In Passing I, 2017
Archival pigment print on silk habotai, custom wood armature

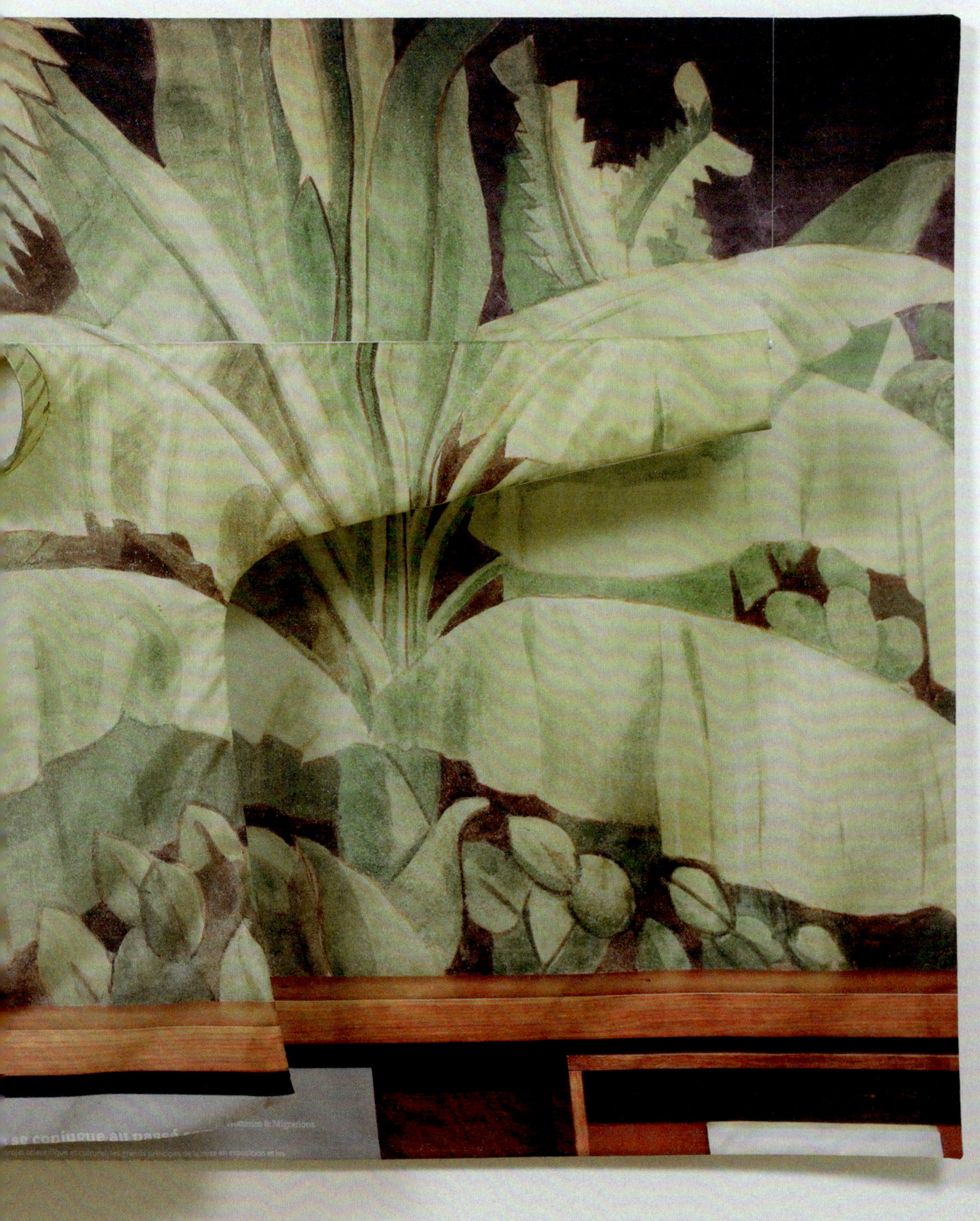

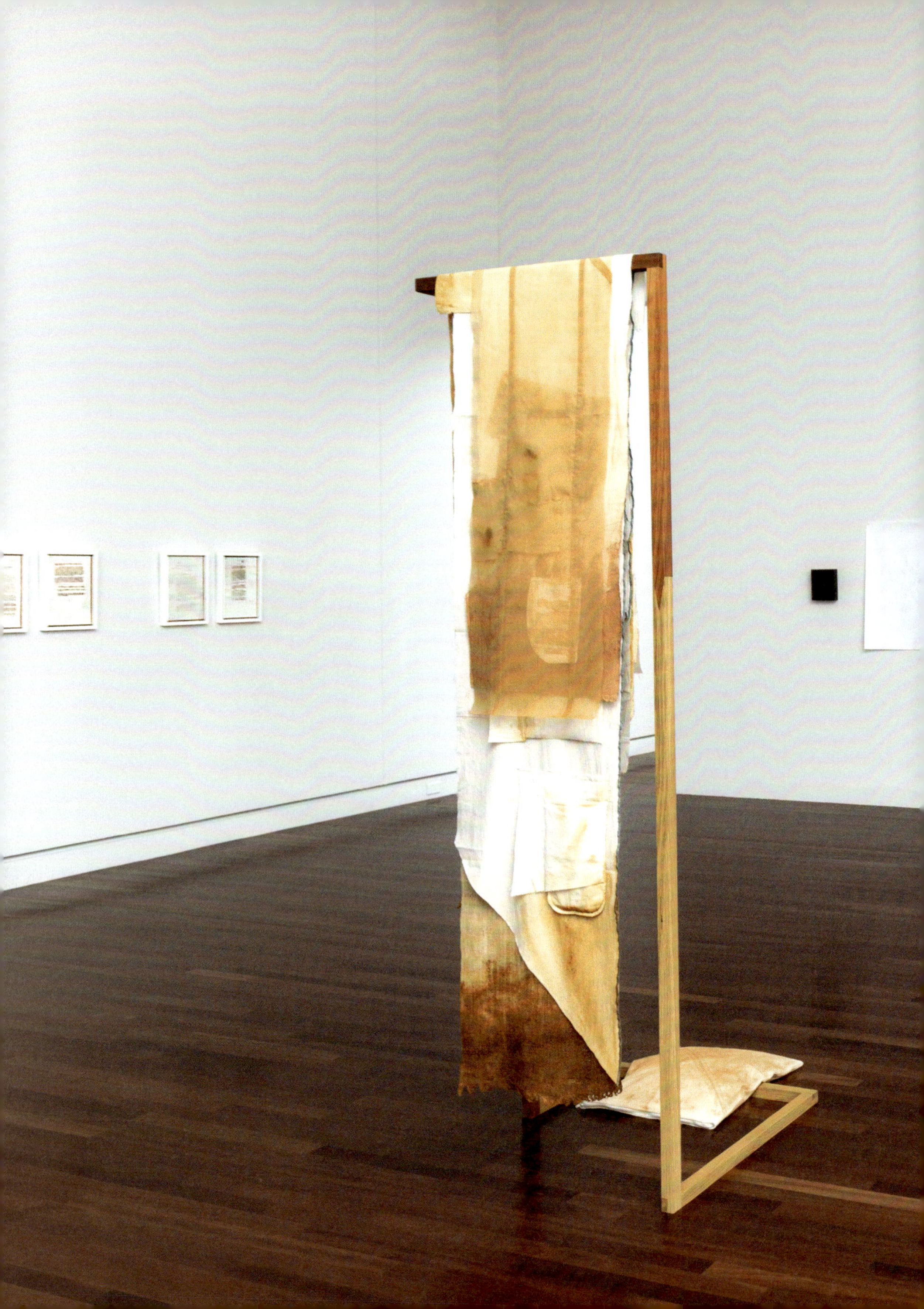

Letter from Nguyễn Thị Minh Khai's father to Marshall Philippe Pétain, 2017
Laser-cut onion skin paper mounted on teak

† If our poor child really committed these faults, it was that she was trained, I assure you.
We refuse to believe that educated as she was, she could really have preached the revolution.

* [illegible] because of our [illegible] insistence that she [illegible] and [illegible] refuse. She was 18. [illegible] that age, a young girl is easy prey for certain unscrupulous individuals

(Pétain – chief of State of Vichy France – Later imprisoned – sentenced to death.)

A Monsieur le Maréchal PÉTAIN

Chef de l'Etat Français

Monsieur le Maréchal,

[illegible] is an unhappy father who comes to ask for your clemency of his daughter condemned to death

C'est un malheureux père qui vient solliciter votre clémence en faveur de sa fille [illegible], condamnée à mort par la Cour Martiale de Saïgon à la suite des événements de Novembre 1940.

Our unfortunate child left our roof ten years ago, in order not to be forced into marriage

Notre malheureuse enfant a quitté notre toit, il y a dix ans, pour ne pas contracter le mariage que nous avions en vue pour elle et c'est devant notre fâcheuse insistance qu'elle s'enfuit et se réfugia en Cochinchine. Elle avait à cette époque 18 ans. A cet âge, une jeune fille est une proie facile pour certains individus peu scrupuleux.

Que s'est-il passé ? Nous n'en savons rien hélas ! n'ayant plus eu de ses nouvelles. What happened? Alas, we have no more news.

It is more probable, if not certain, that she had to be trained by Communist individuals who drove her into a compromise to seek shelter and her feminine weakness failed to resist

Mais il est plus que probable, sinon certain, qu'elle a dû être entraînée par un ou plusieurs individus communistes qui l'auront [illegible] poussée dans cette voie pour la compromettre et s'abriter derrière elle et sa faiblesse de femme n'a pas su résister aux mauvais conseils. Mais nous nous refusons à croire, Monsieur le Maréchal, qu'élevée comme elle l'a été, elle ait pu réellement prêcher la révolte et le sabotage. Petit fonctionnaire, j'ai élevé tous mes enfants dans le respect de leurs parents et des autorités et si notre pauvre enfant a réellement commis des fautes, c'est qu'elle a été entraînée, je puis vous l'assurer. If our poor child really committed these faults, it was that she was [illegible] you.

D'après ce que nous a écrit son Avocat, qui est le Doyen du barreau de Saïgon, elle aurait été condamnée simplement sur le rapport d'un Commissaire de Police et celui d'un jeune expert qui a osé affirmer devant la Cour qu'une brochure intitulée "L'oeuvre de Sabotage" était de la main de notre fille. Or, tout le monde sait qu'il ne faut attacher qu'un crédit très minime aux expertises en écriture, des affaires retentissantes l'ont démontré – Des experts connus du monde entier ont été pris en défaut ; comment avec le peu de moyens dont on dispose à la Colonie, un jeune expert, peut-il être aussi affirmatif ?

Aucun des témoins entendus à l'instruction ne l'a été devant la Cour Martiale ; pourquoi ? Aucun d'eux cependant n'avait reconnu notre fille devant le Magistrat instructeur et malgré cela, la Cour l'a condamnée à la peine capitale !

Ma pauvre femme et moi, n'avons donc plus d'espoir qu'en votre clémence, Monsieur le Maréchal.

C'est un vieux père qui vient vous crier : "Pitié" pour mon enfant et confiant dans la grande bonté de celui qui est à l'heure actuelle le Père de la France et de son Empire, ma femme et moi vous supplions à genoux de faire grâce de la vie à notre malheureuse enfant.

Certains que vous entendrez l'appel fait à votre coeur/de vieux parents éplorés, nous vous prions de bien vouloir agréer, Monsieur le Maréchal, l'hommage de notre plus profond respect et de notre profonde reconnaissance ainsi que l'assurance de notre attachement à la Grande Nation protectrice.

It is an old father who comes to beg you "Pity for our child"

According to our lawyer, she was sentenced to death simply on the report of one.

Letter from Nguyễn Thị Minh Khai to father (Nguyễn Văn Bình), 2017
Laser-cut onion skin paper mounted on teak

[TR]ADUCTION d'une lettre recommandée postée à Hanoi le 24-4-41 [pa]r un nommé BEU à l'adresse de M. NGUYEN VAN BINH, N° [illegible] rue [Ma]réchal Foch à Vinh (Annam).

-:-

Lettre examinée par le C/P. de Hanoi

Acheminement Suspendu

intercepted letter

Hanoi, le 25 Avril 1941

My dear father

*(This request was drafted by the lawyer for her father to ~~[illegible]~~ transcribe.)

Mon cher Père,

Je vous renvoie la requête rédigée par l'avocat, pour que vous la transcriviez de votre main et que vous la signiez. Comme vous l'a conseillé l'avocat, écrivez la tout de suite (faites vous la lire par BUONG), puis dites à BUONG de l'envoyer sous pli recommandé (0$17 ; inutile d'y ajouter un timbre ordinaire) directement au Gouverneur Général. En haut de la requête, mettez :

A Monsieur le Maréchal Chef de l'Etat
(s/c de M. le Gouverneur Général de l'Indochine)

Monsieur le Maréchal,

Etc.....

Copy the original; don't change anything

Rédigez la suivant l'original ; inutile d'y ajouter ou d'y retrancher quoi que ce soit.

J'ai déjà répondu à l'avocat pour le remercier et le prier de me dire :

1°- s'il est possible d'aller rendre visite à K. et quand.

2°- Quand la décision du Maréchal Pétain arrivera ici.

(Pétain - Chief of State of Vichy France Later imprisoned and sentenced to death himself.)

Maintenant que vous êtes fatigué, viendrez-vous à Hanoi ? Si oui, faites-le moi savoir à l'avance, par lettre adressée à

Voie 256, n° 2 (Sinh Tu) HANOI

Vous me direz par la même occasion si je dois adresser une requête pour demander audience au Gouverneur Général, afin que je fasse le nécessaire à l'avance et éviter ainsi tout retard.

J'ai entendu dire que BA était déjà sortie. Cela m'a rendu très triste. Je suis actuellement très occupé. L'examen est proche encore seulement deux semaines, et comme il fait à nouveau chaud, je suis très fatigué.

Si vous venez, ne venez pas directement chez moi, car le propriétaire vous inviterait et cela les dérangerait./.

Signé : BEU --

(She is learning about her grandmother's death in [illegible] prison)

("z" does not exist in Vietnamese.)

Letter from Nguyễn Thị Minh Khai to Comrades or Các Anh (Brothers) (pages 1 and 2), 2017
Laser-cut onion skin paper mounted on teak

comrades imposes equality with the vietnamese

clarifies that she is [illegible] to all men

Traduction d'une lettre manuscrite saisie au cours
de la perquisition effectuée le [illegible] au domicile de
[illegible]
demeurant à Thai Hiep [illegible] (Giadinh)

Il faut [illegible] d'urgence quelqu'un pour [illegible] ...

Camarades !

Pourquoi [illegible] ? Vous n'êtes pas [illegible] [illegible] de rendez-vous. Ce qui [illegible] que le camarade [illegible] (1) [illegible] pendant longtemps, sans que personne ne vînt l'avertir, [illegible] l'emmener. Mais j'ignorais le lieu de rendez-vous et, d'ailleurs je ne recevais pas d'instruction à ce sujet. [illegible] chez le camarade [illegible] (1), mais j'avais peur [illegible] curieux. J'aurais pu assister à la réunion d'aujourd'hui. Bien qu'en dépit de ma présence à cette réunion je n'aurais pas le droit de voter les décisions, mon invitation eût [illegible] conforme au principe.

In spite of my presence at the meeting, I had not the right of vote (she is highest ranking at the time, but not able to vote bc she is a woman)

[illegible], il se passe actuellement des événements d'une gravité exceptionnelle pouvant avoir des répercussions [illegible]. Il faut résoudre cette question [illegible] de la question financière qui est très importante. [illegible] de plusieurs centaines de piastres et attendons [illegible] du Comité Central ou du Comité de pays. Il faut envoyer un [illegible] digne de confiance pour venir les prendre.

[illegible] distribute the work more evenly.

Il sera demandé, en outre, au Comité Central de [illegible] plus nettement les travaux. En effet, parfois nous [illegible] peine sans obtenir aucun résultat, cela à cause de la [illegible] répartition du travail.

Je sais bien que l'idée d'une femme que je suis, même si elle est juste ou empreinte de quelque caractère politique juste, n'inspire pas grand'confiance. Cependant, j'estime que, depuis le jour où j'ai travaillé avec les camarades d'ici, je n'ai pas encore fait de motion ou déclenché une activité qui soit contraire au principe ou à la politique du Parti. Mais qui sait si, aux yeux des autres, mes agissements n'ont pas parfois paru erronés ?

I am aware that I am, even if just or in the world of a political character, does not inspire great confidence

According to some comrades, I had ideas [illegible] individualistic or not inspiring great confidence

D'après quelques camarades, j'ai des idées trop individualistes ou n'inspirant pas de confiance. Je ne m'en formalise point. Mais ce dont je suis navrée, c'est que notre Parti, même les organes dirigeants, garde encore un caractère trop "petit bourgeois".

Il y a aujourd'hui parmi vous un camarade du Comité de ville. Le Comité provincial doit se renseigner auprès de lui pour être fixé sur mes agissements et pour voir si les critiques faites par certains camarades contre moi sont justes ou non.

Que les camarades ne considèrent pas cette question comme ne regardant qu'un individu, car elle pourrait avoir

des ....

(questions of class as secular front takes hold)

i ask that your critiques be severe in the case that my actions are truly blameworthy

- 2 -

des répercussions sur la collectivité. Je demande que vos critiques soient sévères au cas où mes agissements seraient vraiment blâmables.

Je vous demande enfin de confier du travail seulement à ceux qui sont dignes de confiance. Et, à ce sujet, il faut que le travail et les responsabilités soient bien déterminés, car, sans cela, il nous serait très difficile de résoudre les questions urgentes et de mener à bonne fin tout travail important. En ce qui me concerne, que vous ayez ou non confiance en moi, j'ai pleine confiance dans la révolution et dans notre mission dont je suis toujours conscient, [illegible]'au fin fond de mon coeur. Il suffit de se connaître soi-même et de remplir son devoir, l'avenir et la lutte nous fourniront la réponse. Toutefois, que mes camarades se montrent assez scrupuleux avant de prendre une décision quelconque.

Camarades, si j'ai dit plus haut que nos organes dirigeants conservent encore un caractère trop petit-bourgeois, c'est parce que je me suis basé sur mon expérience de ces deux dernières années. Si mes camarades réfléchissent bien, ils feront la même constatation que moi. Les camarades responsables se rangeront aussi à mon raisonnement. Il faut faire de telle sorte que ce vestige (petit-bourgeois) soit supprimé à jamais ./.

---

(1) - L'abréviatif S. doit correspondre au nom d'un camarade "LO" probablement. Le papier est arraché à cet endroit.

(2) - "BA" doit s'identifier avec [illegible] dit BA [illegible] chez qui était installé le siège de l'organe de liaison du parti.

(3) - Cette lettre, par le ton et le [illegible], doit dater [illegible] Indochine, laquelle doit être [illegible] [illegible] dite [illegible] alias LE [illegible].

whether or not you have confidence in me, I have plenty of confidence in the revolution.

Profile of Nguyễn Thị Minh Khai, 2017 (pages 1 and 2)
Laser-cut onion skin paper mounted on teak

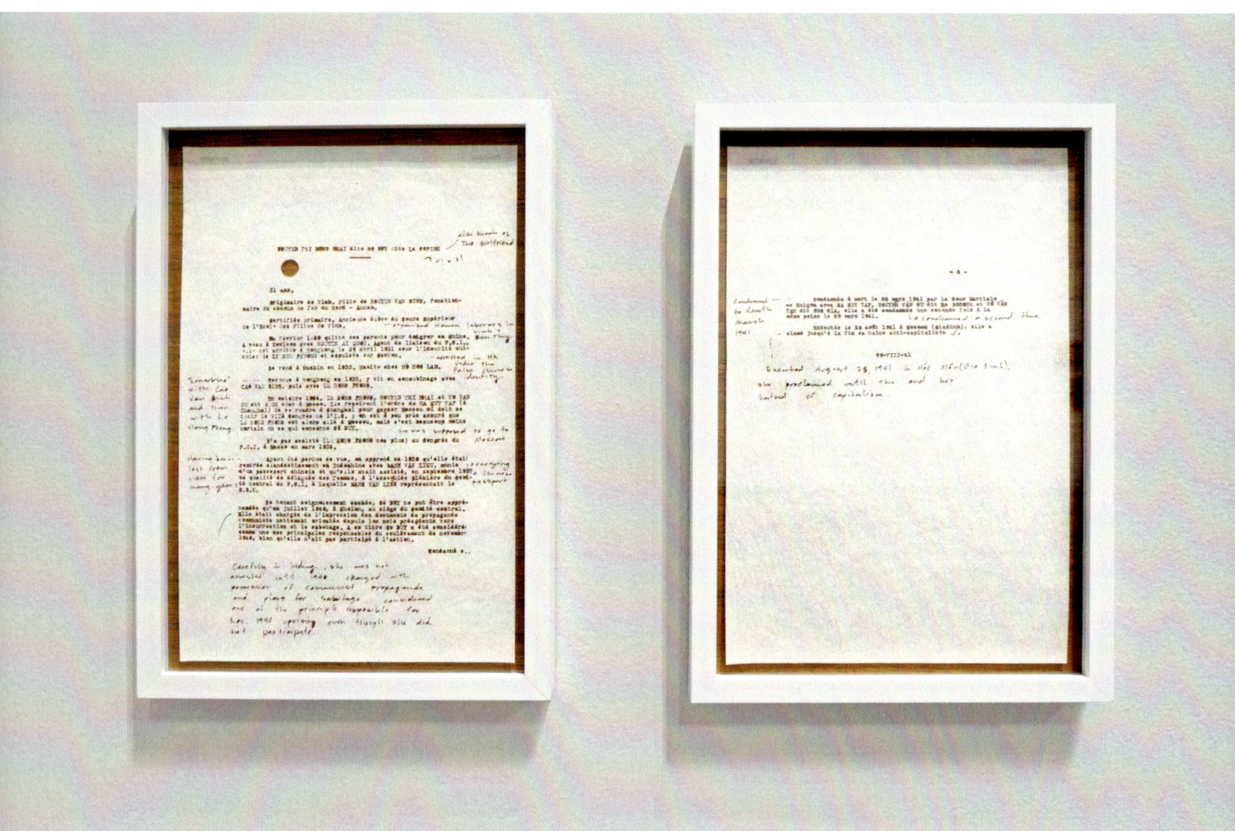

Letters from and about agent "LESQUENDIEU," 2017
Laser-cut onion skin paper mounted on teak

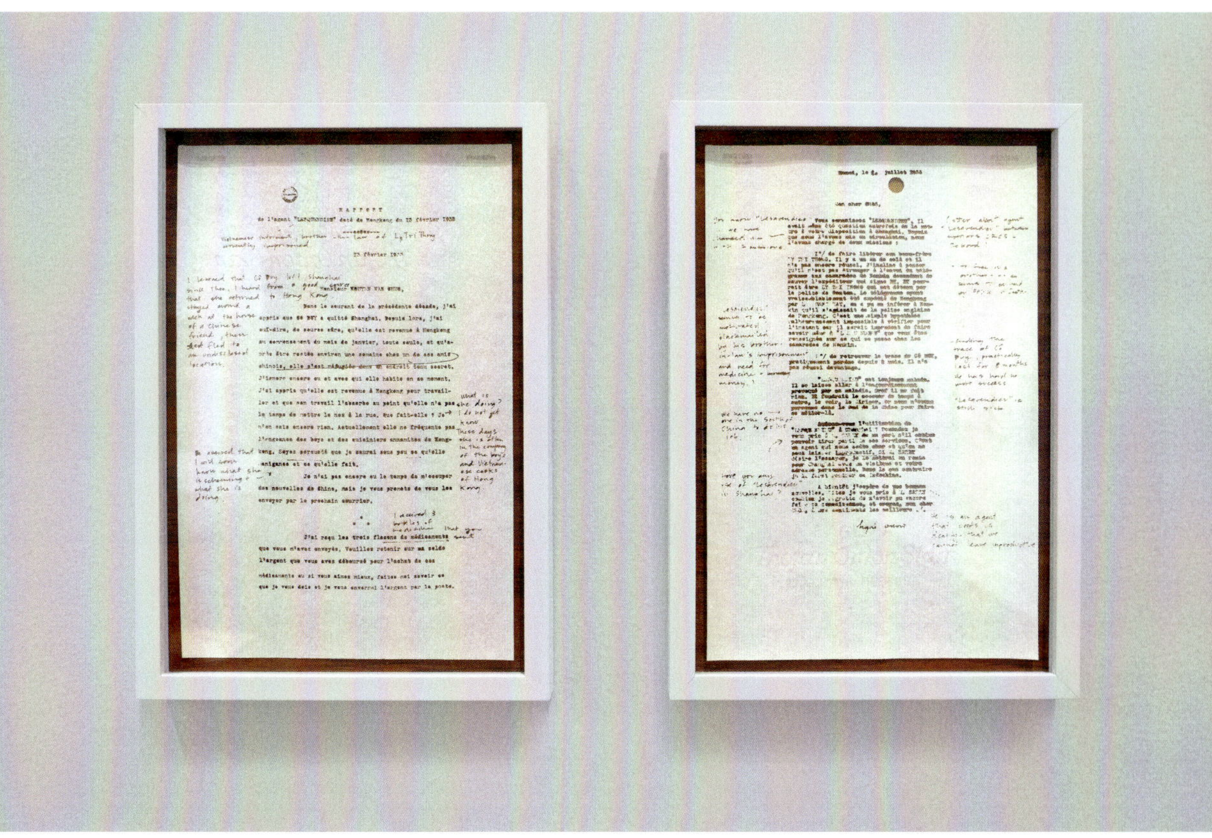

Up Against the State, 2017
Invisible ink on paper, iodine

Da/Skin (I, II), 2024
Stitched handmade dó paper

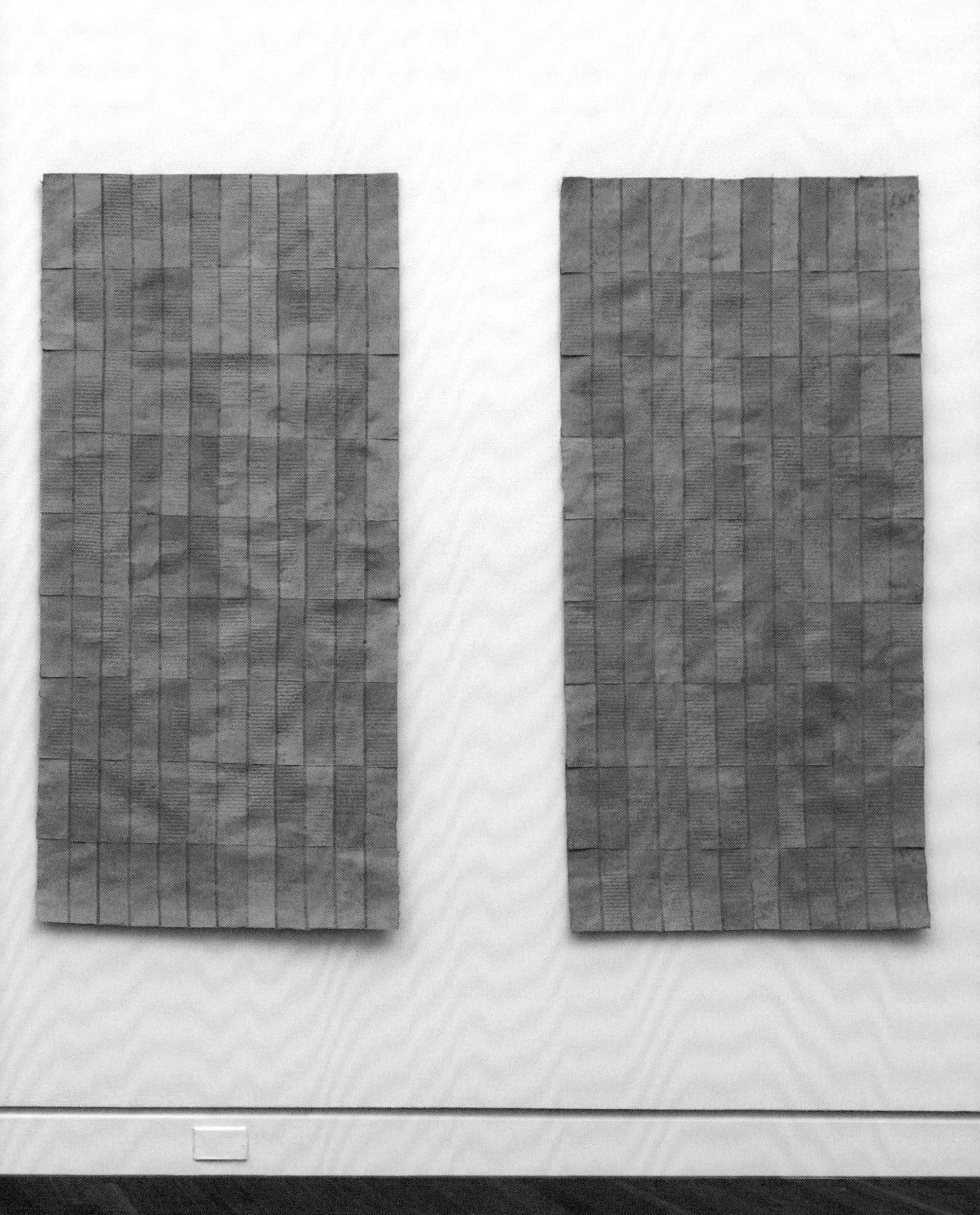

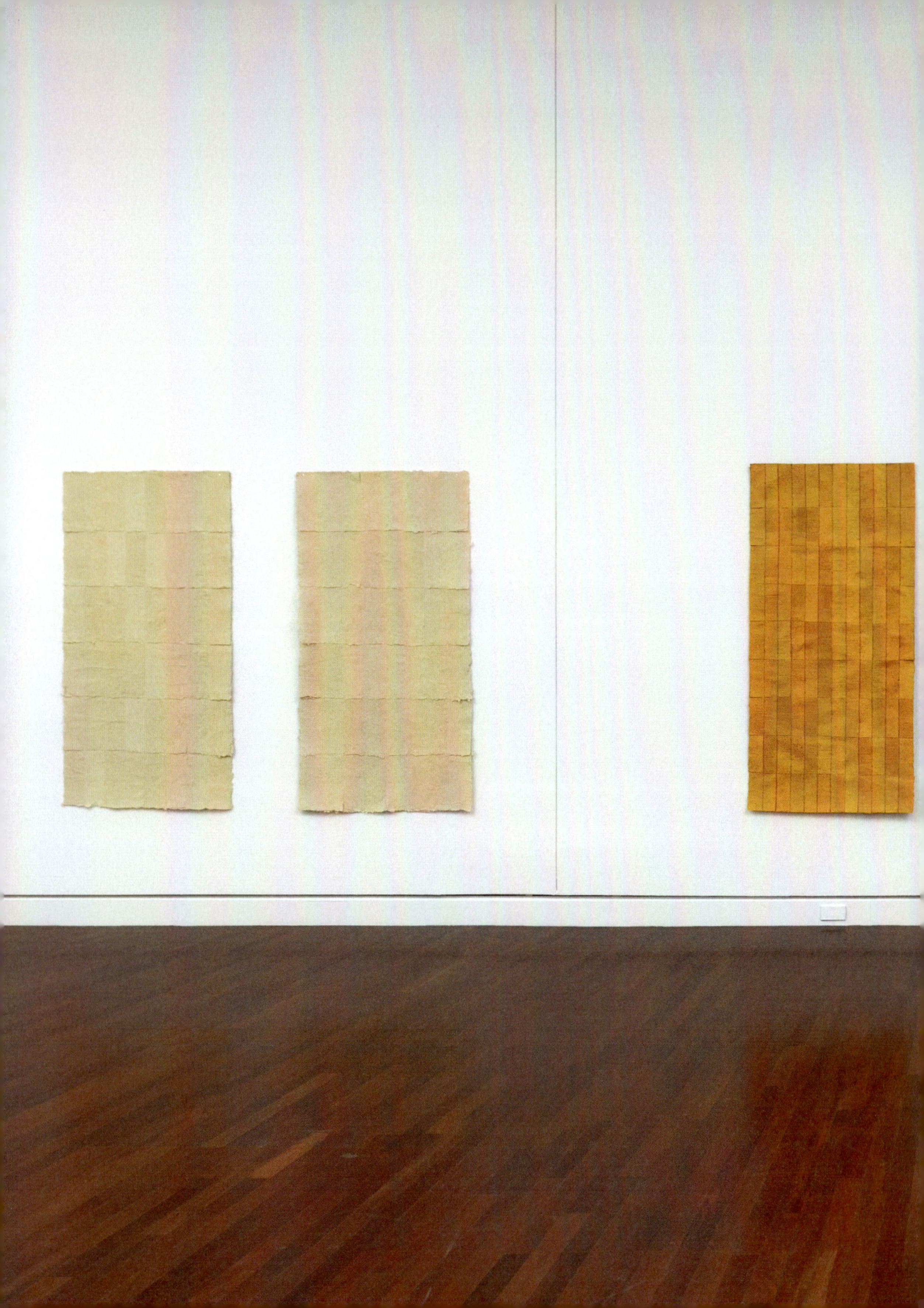

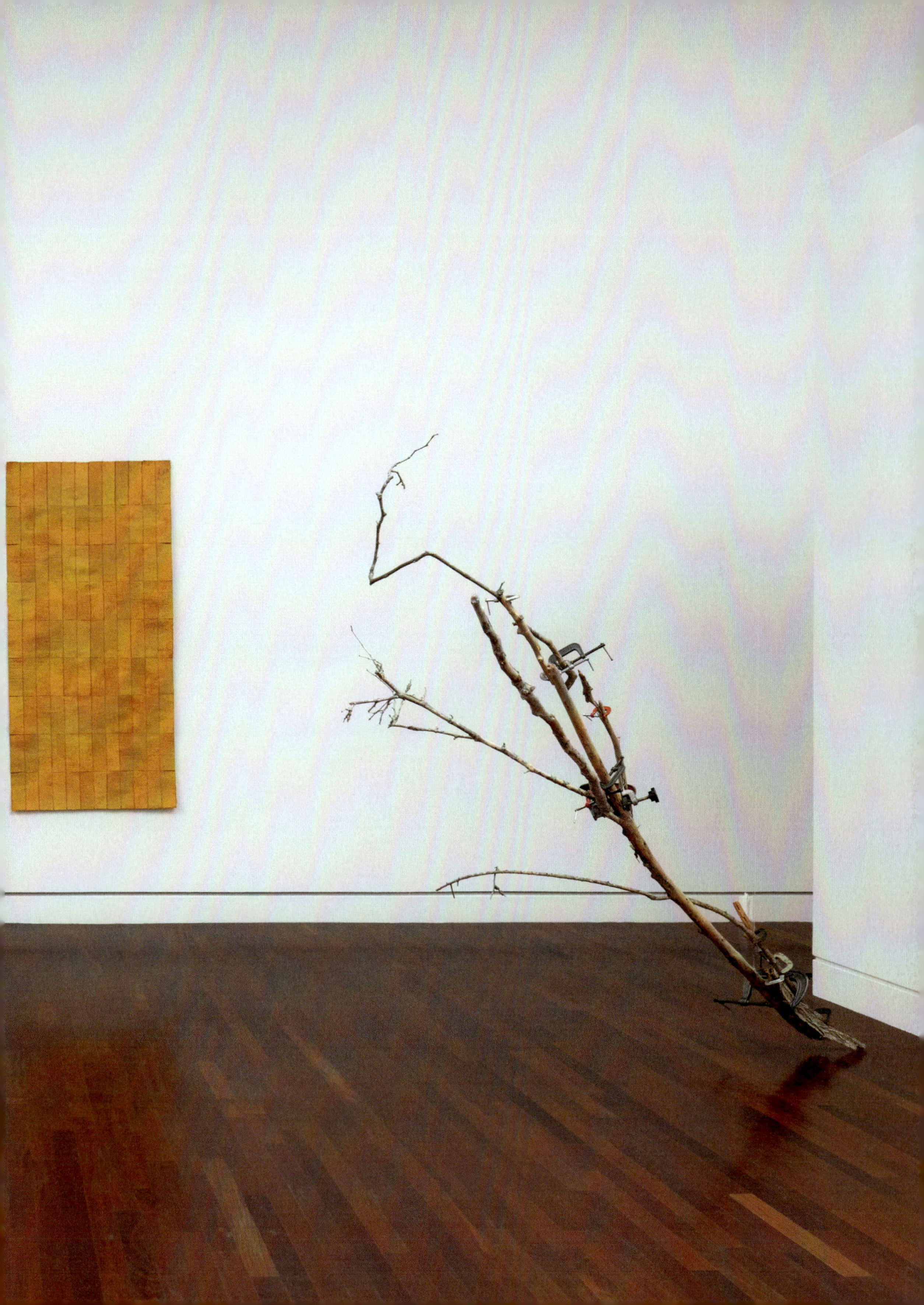

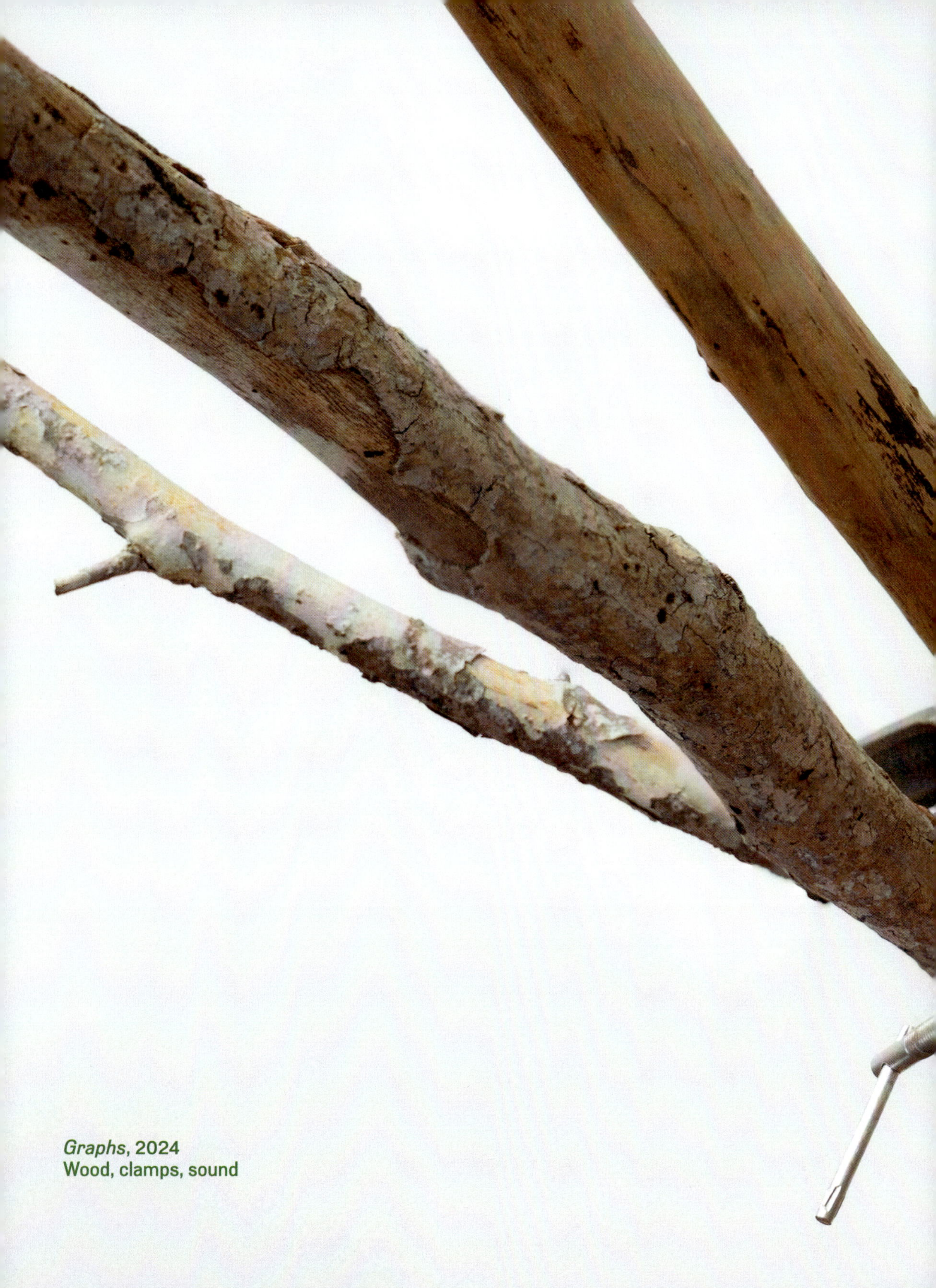

Graphs, 2024
Wood, clamps, sound

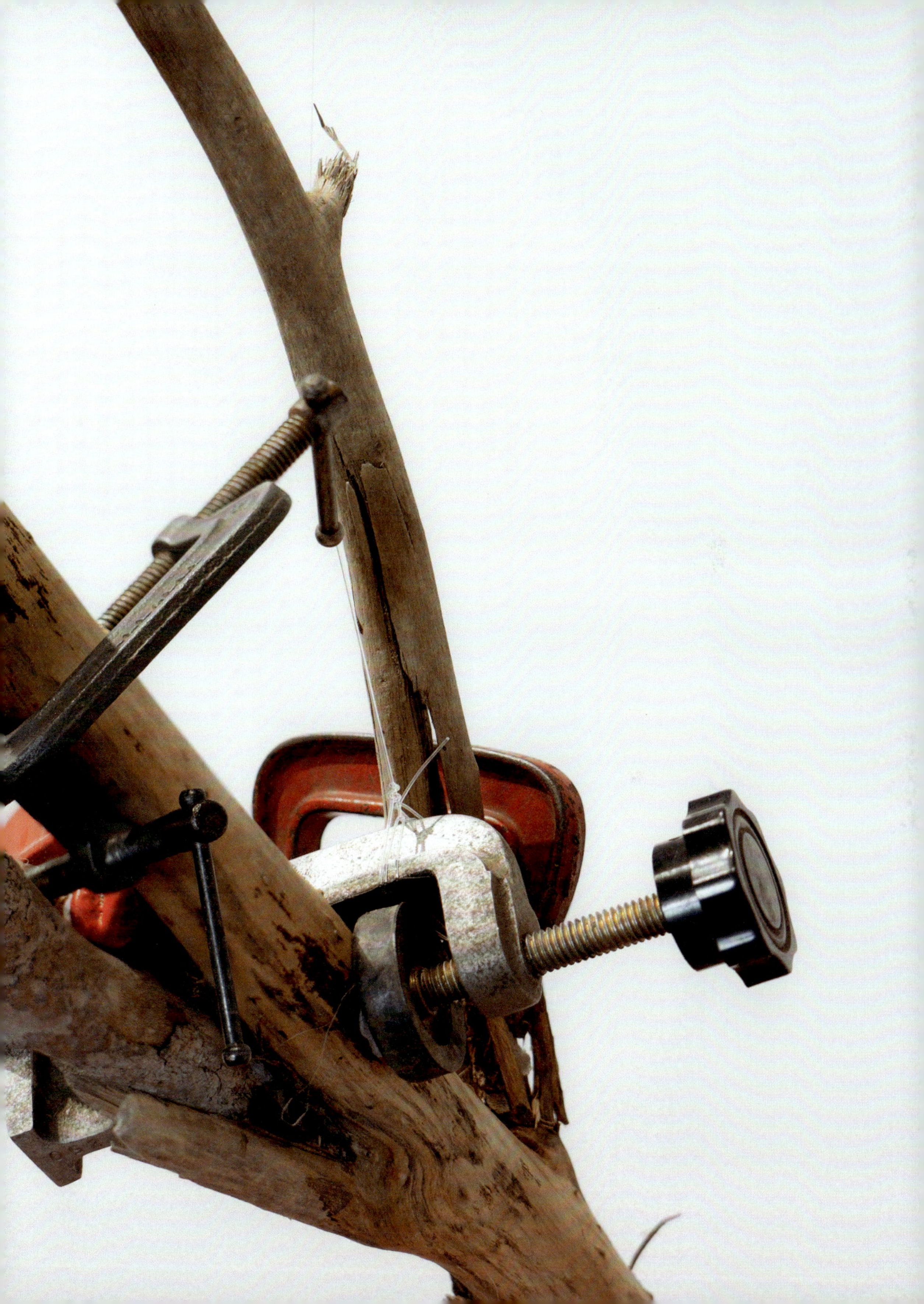

CONTESTING SITES OF (KNOWLEDGE) PRODUCTION

A CONVERSATION BETWEEN ALINE LO & HƯƠNG NGÔ

AL My initial question for you is how refugee knowledge or a refugee epistemology orients you within the colonial archives.[1] And, particularly for this project, the colonial photographs.

HN I think the first aspect is just having a different level of empathy toward the subjects that I'm viewing. There is some desire to see yourself, your family, or your community in the archives. But what you're seeing are people in terrible situations where they aren't really themselves; they're actually showing you the conditions in which they are in. What you are finding instead is a representation of the colonial system. At the same time, as somebody with a personal connection to the material, you have the desire and the patience to look longer. It's more like pointing to the gaps, what is unspoken.

AL What you're saying about patience helps me make sense of my own questions about longing and desire. There's the separation, but also a throughline when visiting the colonial archive with refugee knowledge, and empathy and patience is a really helpful way to frame what's happening.

HN There's an attunement to different details as well. The long-term project I've been working on before this is on Nguyễn Thị Minh Khai and the group of women that were part of the resistance against French colonial rule, and the kind of surveillance that was enacted on them. When I did find photographs, which was very rare, I would gravitate towards certain details that might not be significant to others. There's a picture of Nguyễn Thị Minh Khai that is so strikingly like my grandmother that it really stuck with me. And it's really just because she does her hair in the same way, and she's wearing the same clothes that I remember my grandmother wearing. So, when I'm looking through these colonial plantation photographs, I'm also looking at these little details that for somebody else might not really be significant or register in a different way.

AL These particular photographs, for this exhibit, you chanced upon in a way. What spoke to you about them?

HN The photos from the plantation were absent of much context except that they were photographed by René Tetard for Albert Sarraut, the Governor General of Indochina at that time. With research, I pieced together that they were probably from a *jardin d'essai* (trial garden) where they tested different plants from France or other colonies to see if they could thrive in different environments with the end goal of engineering monocultures that could be grown predictably for export. They were also very likely propaganda for the Marseilles Colonial Exposition of 1922 to entice more farmers to come to Indochina as colonists.

But aside from that, it was just this really strange relationship where the labels described the trees, but the figures were never acknowledged. It seemed to speak volumes about what they might be experiencing in their silence. The way in which they were kind of shrinking back and trying not to be visible, I just sensed a kind of restlessness that I couldn't articulate. Sites like that were perfect grounds for migrant workers to spread revolutionary ideas and understand shared experiences around their dispossession.

AL Do you think you're doing some of that "unmasking" work in this show by creating new objects that more explicitly reveal the system of colonization?

HN Yeah, hopefully. There's the transformation or translation into materials that has been a way for me to learn and share this history. Materials are how I interact with the world. It's how I research and how as an artist, I tell

1 This question is indebted to Ma Vang's *History on the Run: Secrecy, Fugitivity, and Hmong Refugee Epistemologies* (Durham, NC: Duke University Press, 2021).

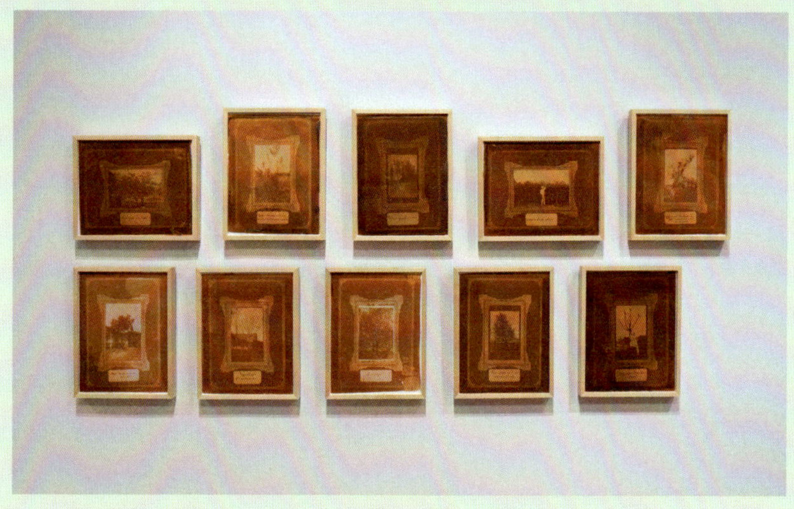

Latent Images (Grafts), 2024. Van Dyke print on paper.

stories. I'm wanting the materials to do as much of that work as possible. Sometimes it's through the materials misbehaving like the Van Dyke prints. They're unfixed so they're constantly changing.

Other works in the exhibition are made with iron that is rusted and will continue to rust. Iron is constantly wanting to return to its natural state of rust, and mine is accelerated because of the way that I treat it. The copper is doing something similar, and both are referencing the extractive industries like mining that came with colonization. These materials are giving you a little bit of that story, but also not staying still; they're misbehaving and disrupting that typical archival process and those conditions.

AL So much of the archive is based on preservation and keeping materials pristine and limiting access because of that. And your work lets the material degrade, which helps us think about the instability of colonial knowledge. I want to keep thinking about process and ask if there are other elements of creating the work that help you figure things out?

HN Yeah. I'm thinking of works that were inspired by archival research, like the invisible ink for the piece *Up Against the State*, which is made by boiling rice, and hectographs, prints that use agar agar as a printing plate. Both of those are forms that you would most easily do in the kitchen. And it required going through the process of making those objects and noticing how they differentiate from other mark-making methods that it clicked for me: these are made in very domestic, gendered spaces. That helped me backtrack and think how these gendered spaces are already political, and brought a nuance to some of the histories of the anticolonial resistance.

There are also a series of blind embossings in the exhibition that are derived from instructional images from some of the first books about grafting. Because they are blind embossed the result is a surface instead of an instructional diagram. They tap into the desire to touch, which I love to evoke in my work. New works are large panels made of handmade dó paper, which has been made in Vietnam for centuries. It's a really tactile paper, fluffier than others. I've been sewing [sheets of it] into these large surfaces that evoke paper and bark and skin at the same time. There's something about all of those surfaces merging together that's really exciting and tantalizing.

So partly I'm researching to find myself in those archives, but then also to create spaces of freedom within my studio where I can then make pieces that aren't necessarily coming from the archives, but are connected in some way.

AL That movement away from the archive brings me to ask how your work is redirecting that imperial gaze, specifically in how Tina Campt thinks about archived colonial photos as compelled, though the ones you use seem beyond compelled.[2]

HN As the official colonial photographer, Tétard is probably still thinking about creating a good photograph, even if it's just for a government commission. But I do feel like the presence of the figures is this strange afterthought. They're asked to be there, either for scale or to focus the cameras. It would seem like they would know they're not really the focus and can do whatever they want with their body and their face. So there's this interesting situation in which they can pose freely. Nevertheless, there's a tension that Campt elaborates on, in the muscles, the gesture, the gaze. The whole album also feels like a strange afterthought. I think it was important at that time for recruiting French farmers but, in the scope of the entire archive, it's not very important. So it's very much possible that these photographs could disappear.

A lot of the documents that I have worked on before are not being digitized because they're not part of "major" histories. We think of the archive as being this permanent space, but materials get reorganized, deaccessioned. Digitization often erases important context information, notes, and captions. So, my work is not necessarily a duplication of what is in the archive, but it's like when you take a plant, cut it, and then start a new plant from it; it's a propagation from the archive. My own archive takes pieces here and there, adding to it from other works that are from the same period, like popular novels, poems, or other documents that were in larger distribution. So sometimes I think of them as these parallel archives or as one archive ungrafting from another.

AL In this way of ungrafting and revising you're not trying to restore or revive the archive. Instead, by being patient and listening in a different way, you're able to create new things or be inspired to create something new. Could you talk more about that, because I think it is such a challenge to create something without simply reviving the archive? How do you think your work finds that balance to reveal the original erasure and the many layers of erasure and violence?[3]

HN Part of my motivation is to simply create space where we look at archival documents differently. Reprinting the photographs points back to the archive and its archival existence, but it is highlighting the figure, rather than the trees.

The prints are always in the process of fading, so it's also a way for these images to have a new life and then to not be visible anymore. So there's this acknowledgement of both a right to be visible as the laborer behind these orchards, and to not be visible, to not need to continually perform as the colonial subject. Saidiya Hartman's text has been really helpful because it does acknowledge absences in this work we're doing. It creates that space to be an artist in these archives, to do these material experiments that allow for speculation.

2 Tina Campt, *Listening to Images* (Durham, NC: Duke University Press, 2017).

3 This question is indebted to Saidiya Hartman's text "Venus in Two Acts," specifically her discussion of "critical fabulation" as a creative act that works " with and against the archive"; *Small Axe* 26, no. 12.2 (June 2008), 12.

AL I think her piece pushes us to hold ourselves accountable for how we create from the archive, which allows us to not be frozen by the archive, or beholden to it.

HN It opens a way of reading the images that gives agency back to those figures in some way. Taking from Campt, what are the acts of refusal that we just can't see because we might only be reading them as subjects of colonization? I lean toward keeping the archival object and recontextualizing it because I have seen when history has been erased and that is not serving in the way that I think that we want it to; we're not able to repeatedly look back and see with nuance.

AL Your work also reminds us how land is colonized too. And it made me think about a refugee's relationship to resettlement, particularly in colonial settler nations. I don't think there's a way to completely reckon with it, but we can start by looking at the institutions we contribute to. I know I make my livelihood through an institution that was founded on the removal of Indigenous people. And the museum is also part of that history. I'm really curious about how you navigate those spaces and how you show your work within those spaces.

HN These are contested territories of knowledge production. They are sites of nation building and ideology formation. Part of my work is to introduce doubt and bring instability into these types of institutional spaces. At the same time, those are places I have learned from. I've spent time in them, I've been sheltered in them.

AL I feel that way about the classroom: a problematic space that has also nurtured me. And I feel a little bit that way about the archive, mostly in that they are both spaces that we transform by both being in them and by creating in spite of them. Sometimes that's not enough, but I think it's something.

HN I wanted to return to your question about settling into a colonial settler nation. At some point during this project, I realized that I was looking for a Vietnamese person of Kinh ethnicity because that is the origin of my mother's family. When I was looking through these photos, I realized that I hadn't really been attending to, first of all, the history of Vietnam as a settler colonial country, but also to the ethnic minorities who are also documented in the archives.

So, for this show there have been moments when it was really important to me to make sure that I include and acknowledge that shared history. As an American, part of my archive work is finding these histories that shed light on the violence enacted on Indigenous peoples in the United States. It's not equating them, but drawing connections to shared histories. And, understanding that narratives that are sometimes decolonial, are also working to divide some of us, like the way that Vietnamese national narrative works to divide the Kinh from ethnic minorities. How might those nationalist narratives that might have been important for us at some time, be reevaluated?

AL I like this idea of shared histories, finding connections, and appreciate how your work is forcing us to confront that need for reevaluation.

One of the joys of being a scholar is that I have the privilege to sort through some things. Not to find solutions or perfect answers, but to talk, think, to write through, or read someone else's work. I'm not sure what else to do with these really complicated feelings and questions that come out of being refugees.

It feels never-ending, which is, I guess, good for us.

HN [Laughs] Yeah, for better or worse.

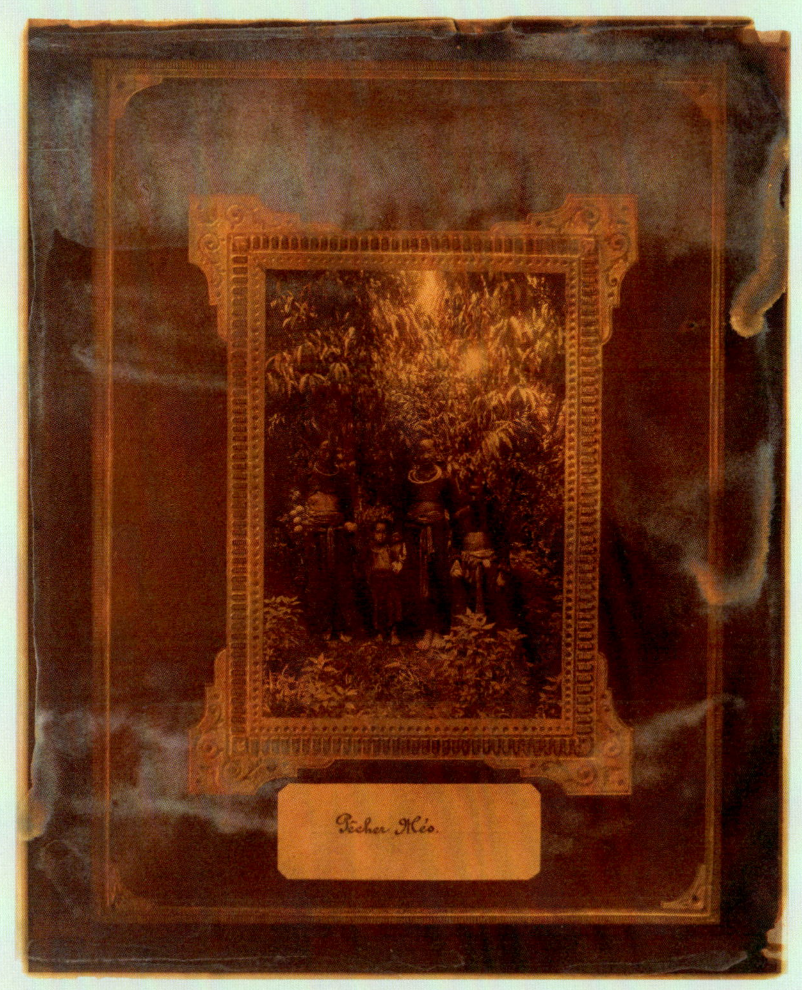

Latent Images (Grafts), 2024. Van Dyke print on paper.

Studies for Ungrafting, 2024
Blind-embossed Rives
BFK paper

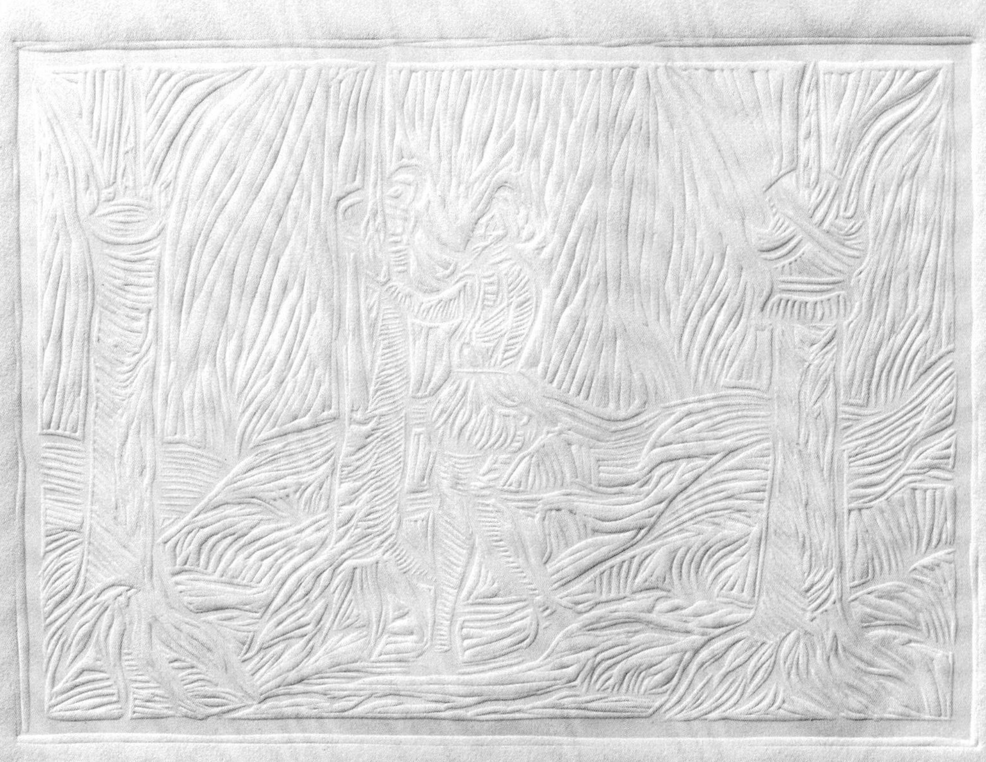

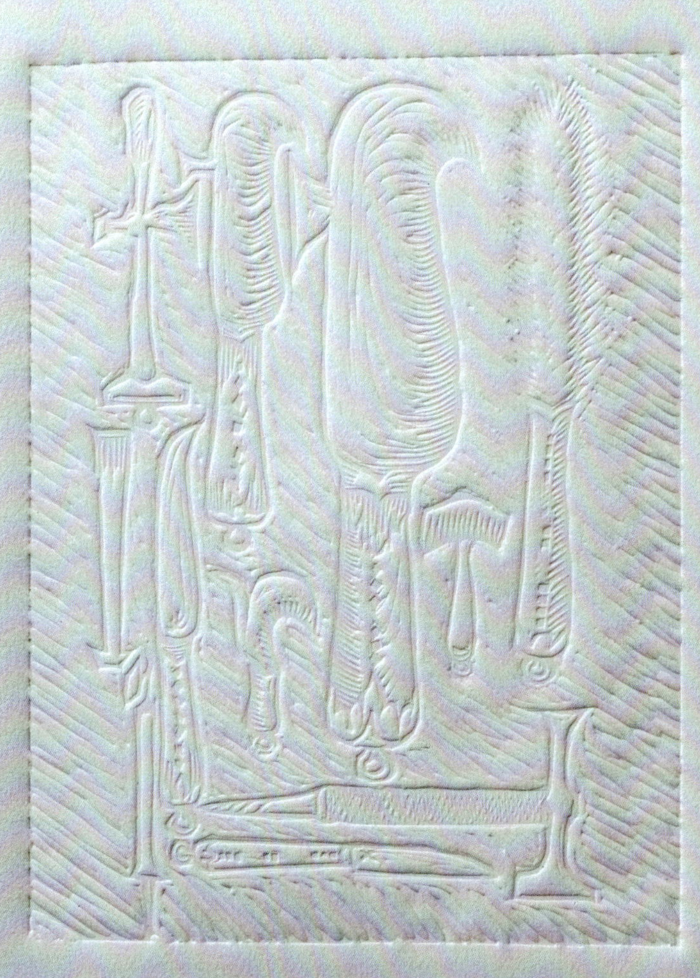

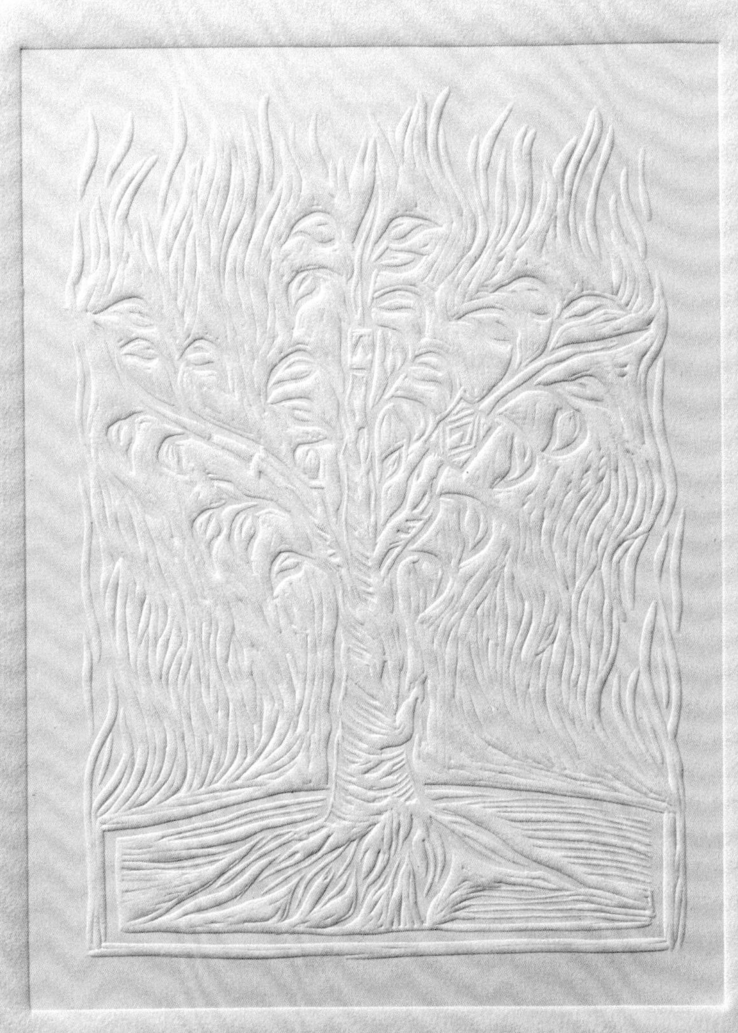

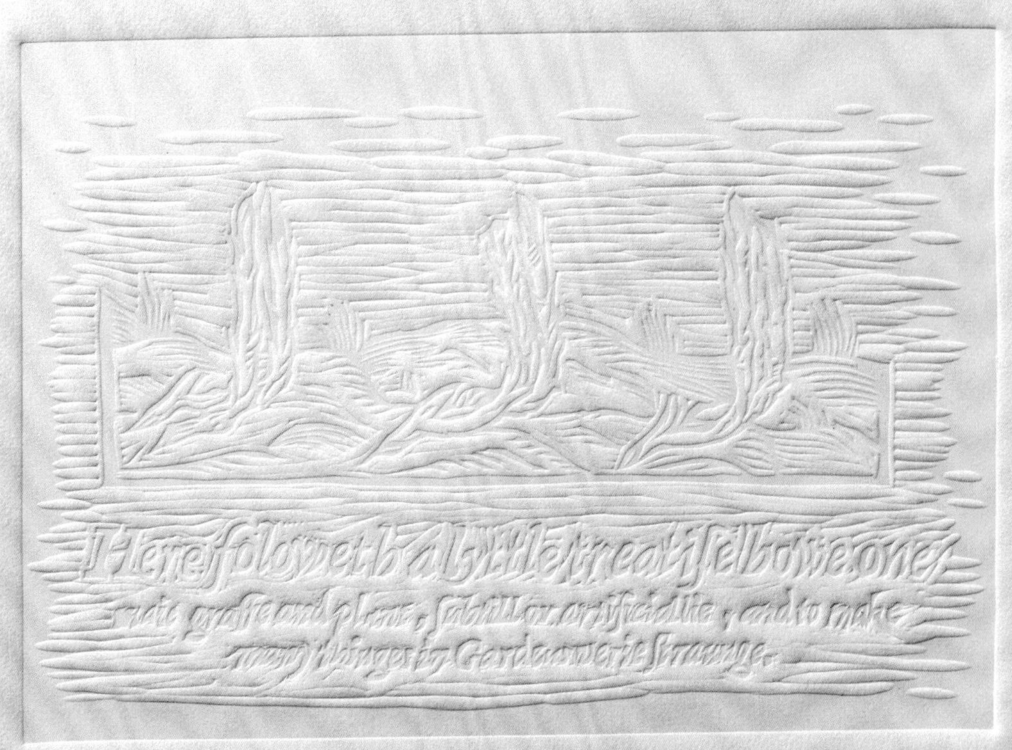
Here foloweth a lyttle treatyse howe one
maie graffe and plante, subtill or artificialie, and to make
many thinges by Gardenwerke straunge.

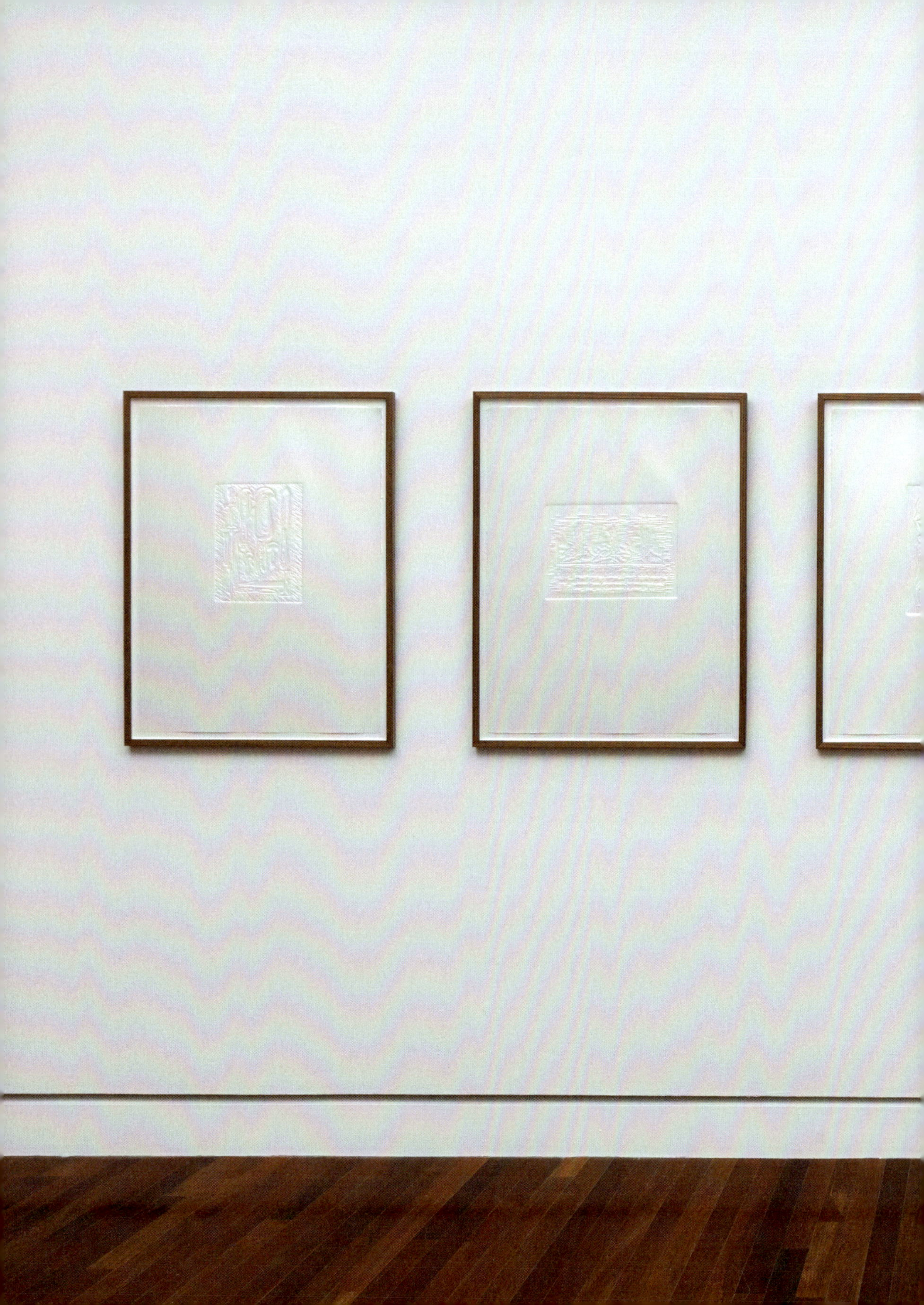

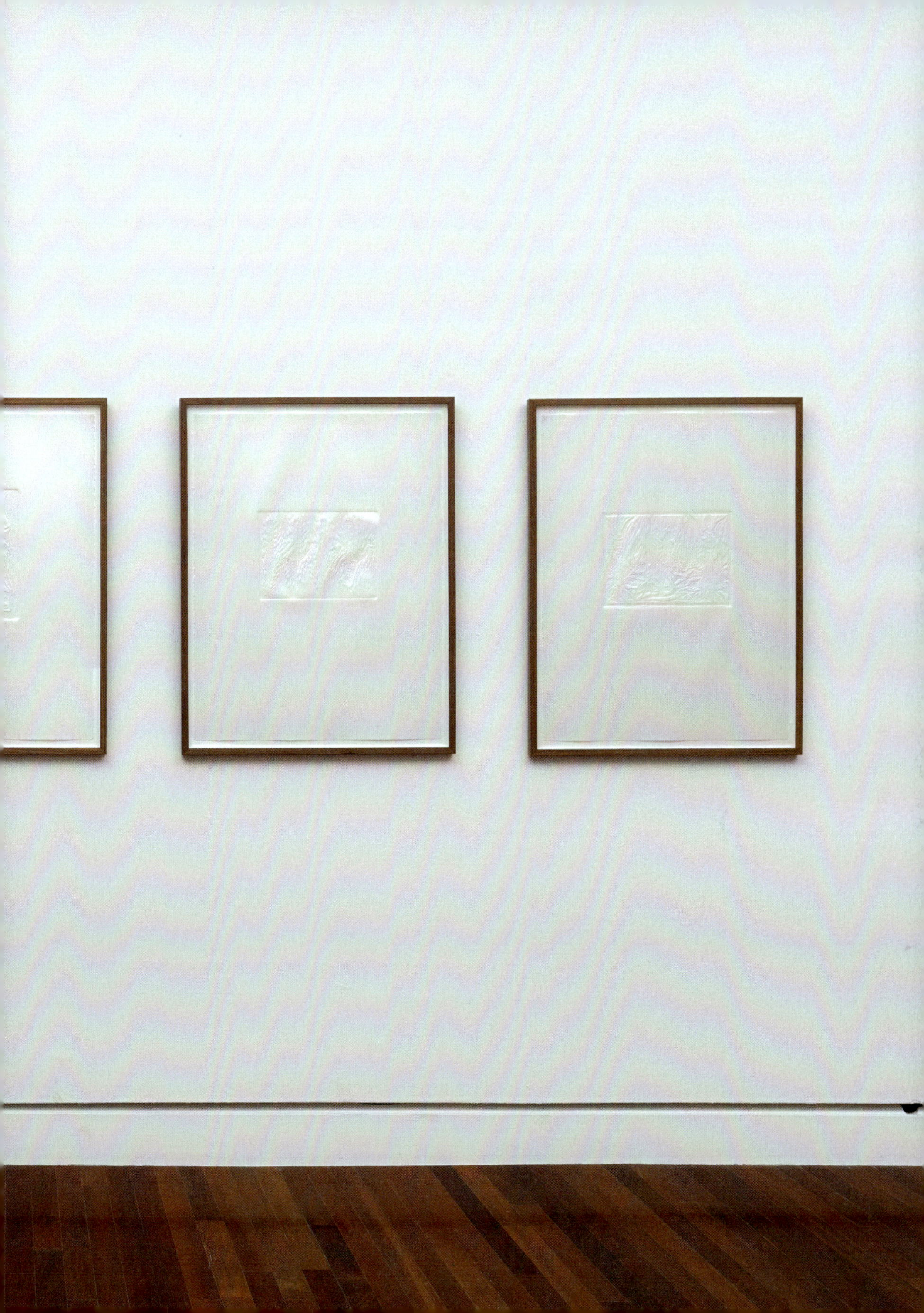

Studies for Translations, 2024
Reproductions of herbarium specimens and plants in LECA (lightweight, expanded clay aggregate)

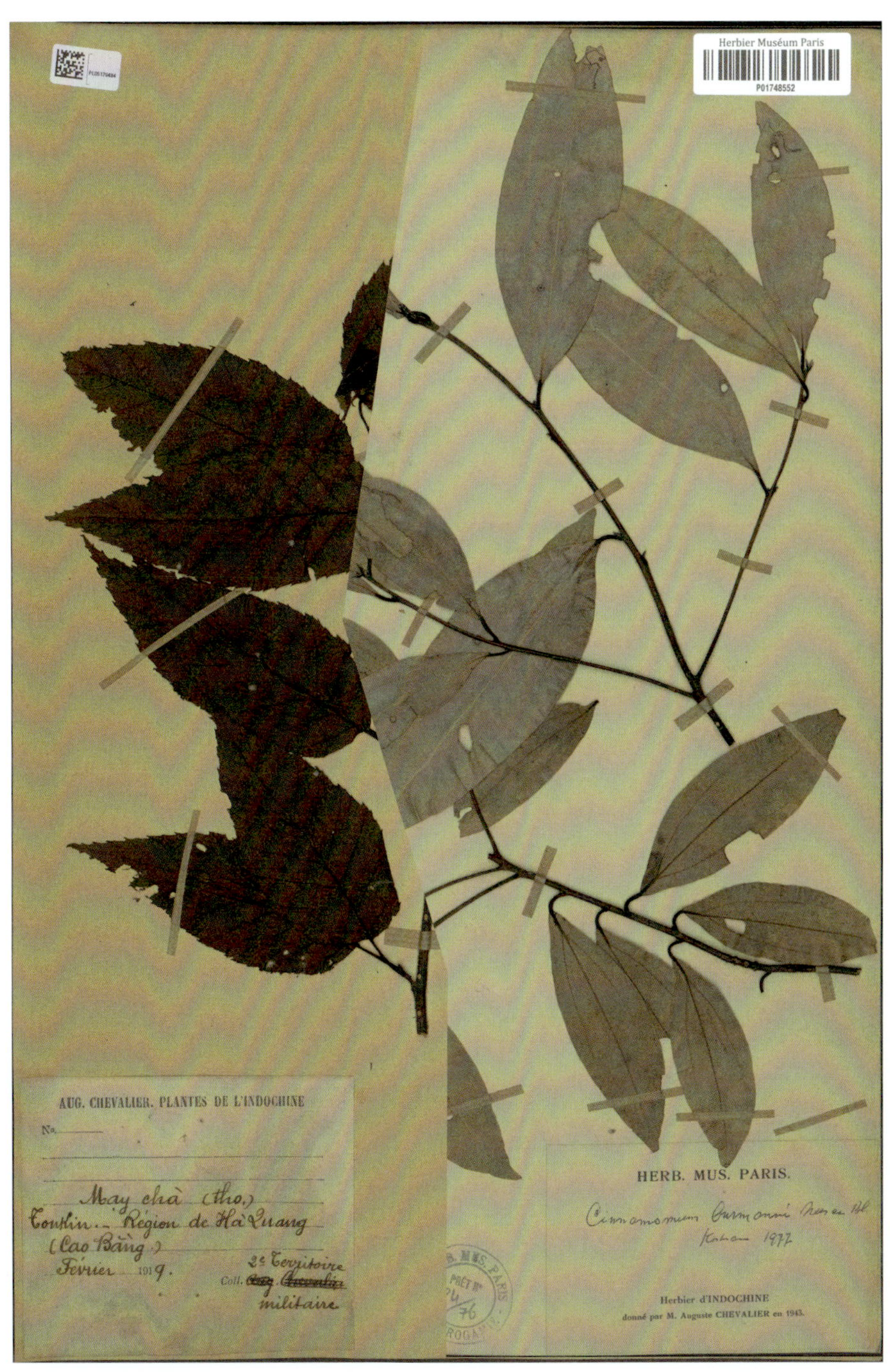
Herbier Muséum Paris
P01748552
AUG. CHEVALIER. PLANTES DE L'INDOCHINE
No
May chà (tho.)
Tonkin.– Région de Hà Quang
(Cao Bàng.)
Février 1919.
Coll. 2e Territoire militaire
HERB. MUS. PARIS.
Herbier d'INDOCHINE
donné par M. Auguste CHEVALIER en 1943.

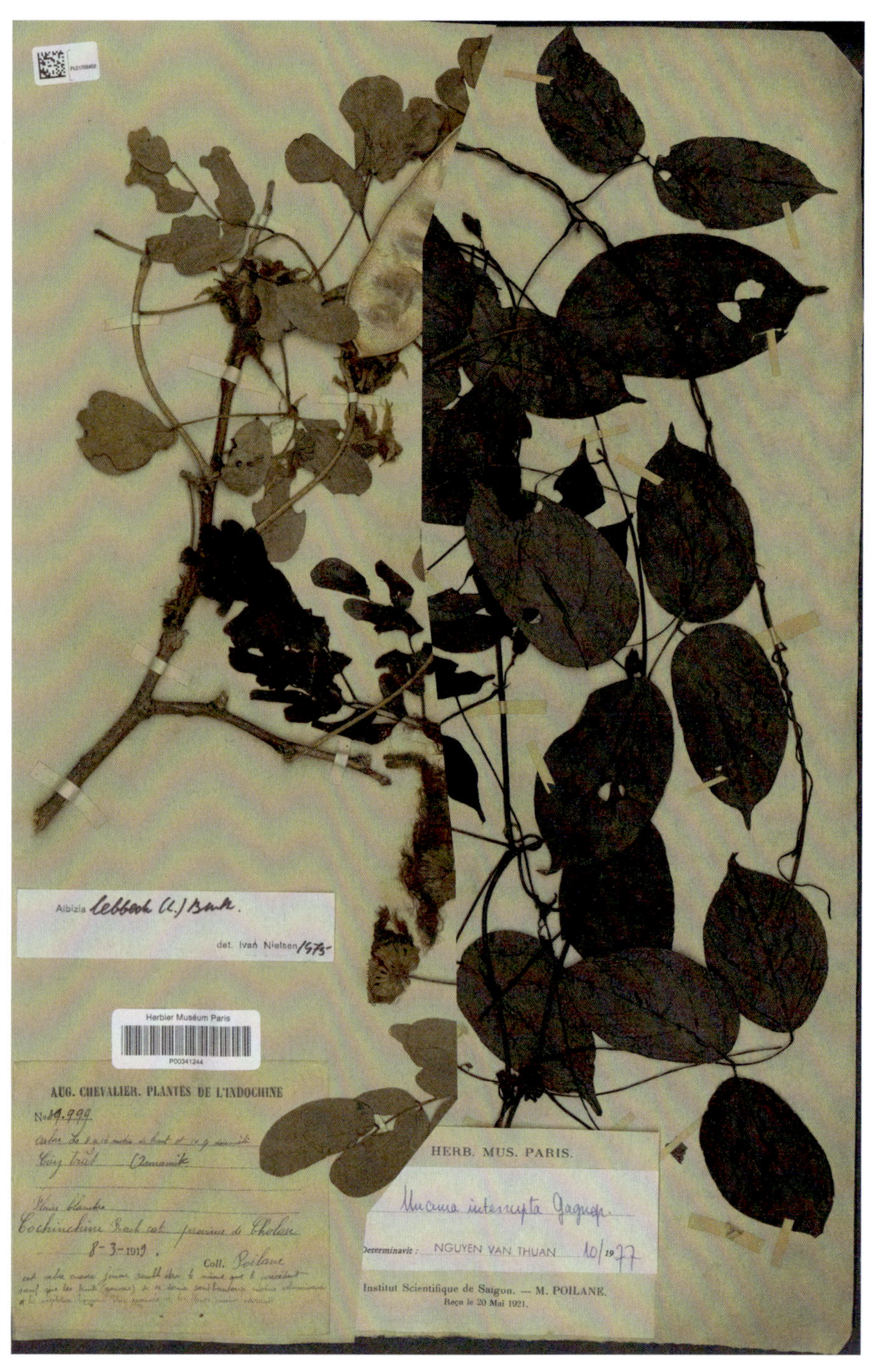

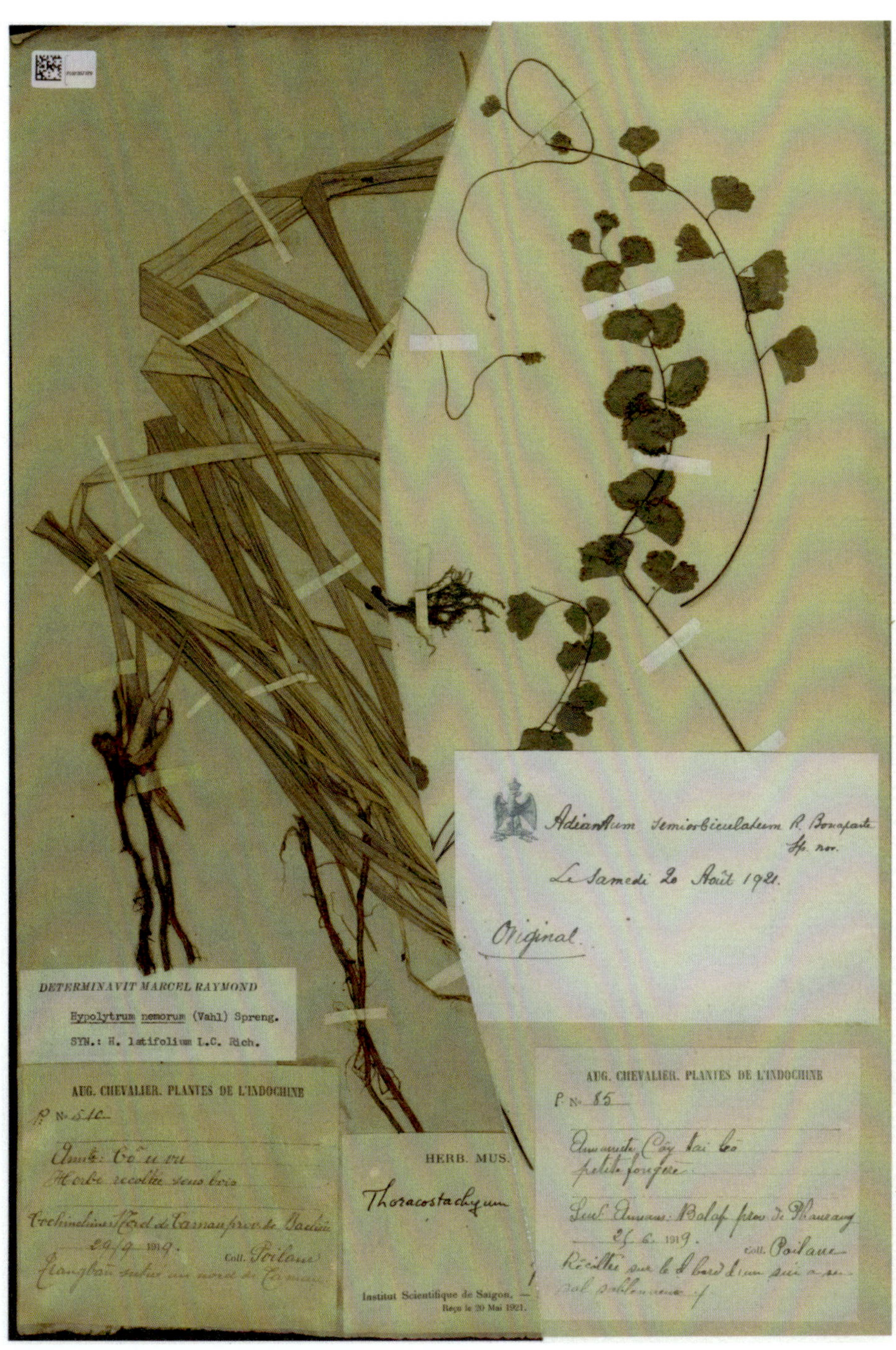

Adiantum semiorbiculatum R. Bonaparte
sp. nov.
Le Samedi 20 Août 1921.
Original.
DETERMINAVIT MARCEL RAYMOND
Hypolytrum nemorum (Vahl) Spreng.
SYN.: H. latifolium L.C. Rich.
AUG. CHEVALIER. PLANTES DE L'INDOCHINE
AUG. CHEVALIER. PLANTES DE L'INDOCHINE
HERB. MUS.
Thoracostachyum
Institut Scientifique de Saigon,
Reçu le 20 Mai 1921.

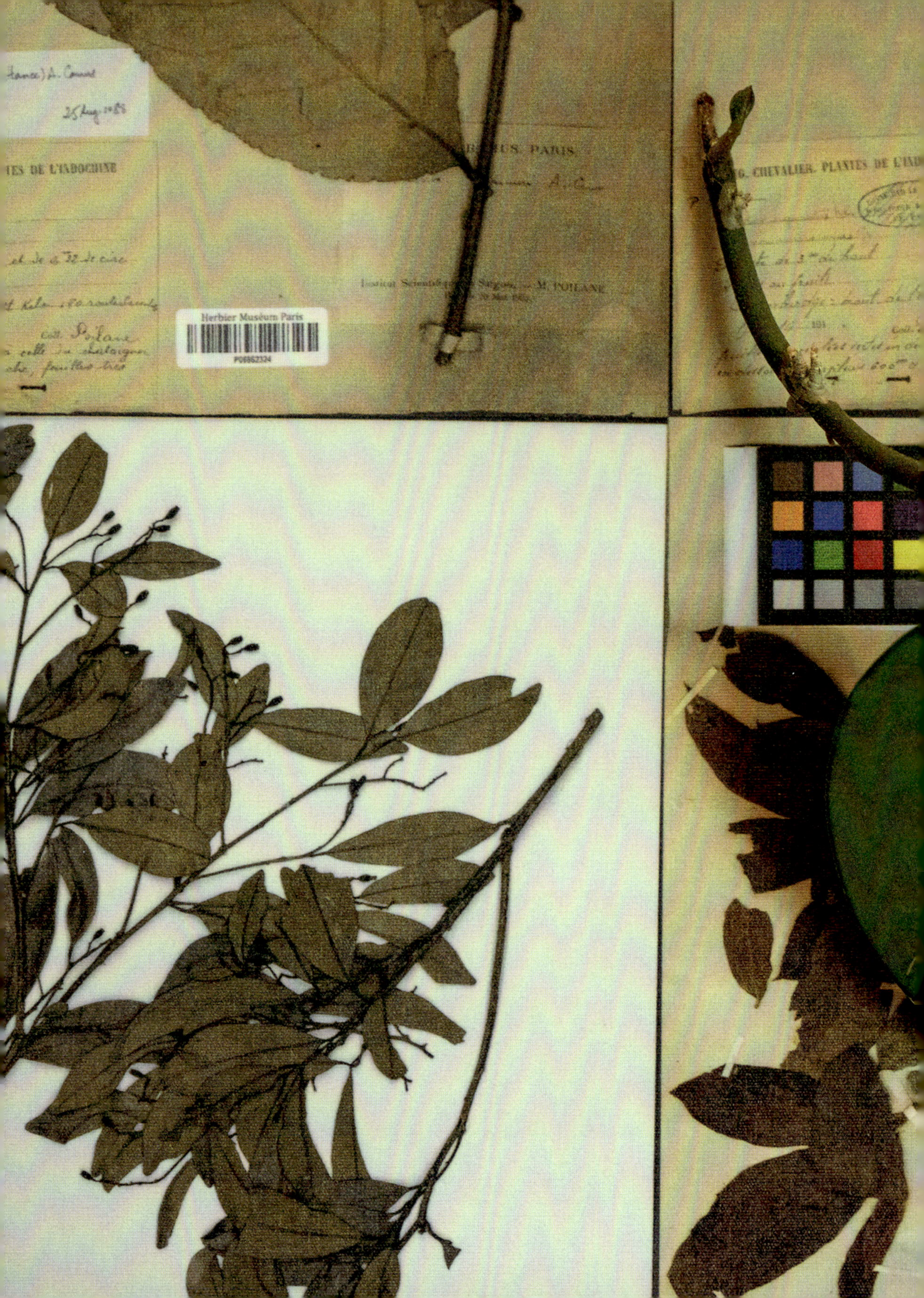
Herbier Muséum Paris
M. POILANE

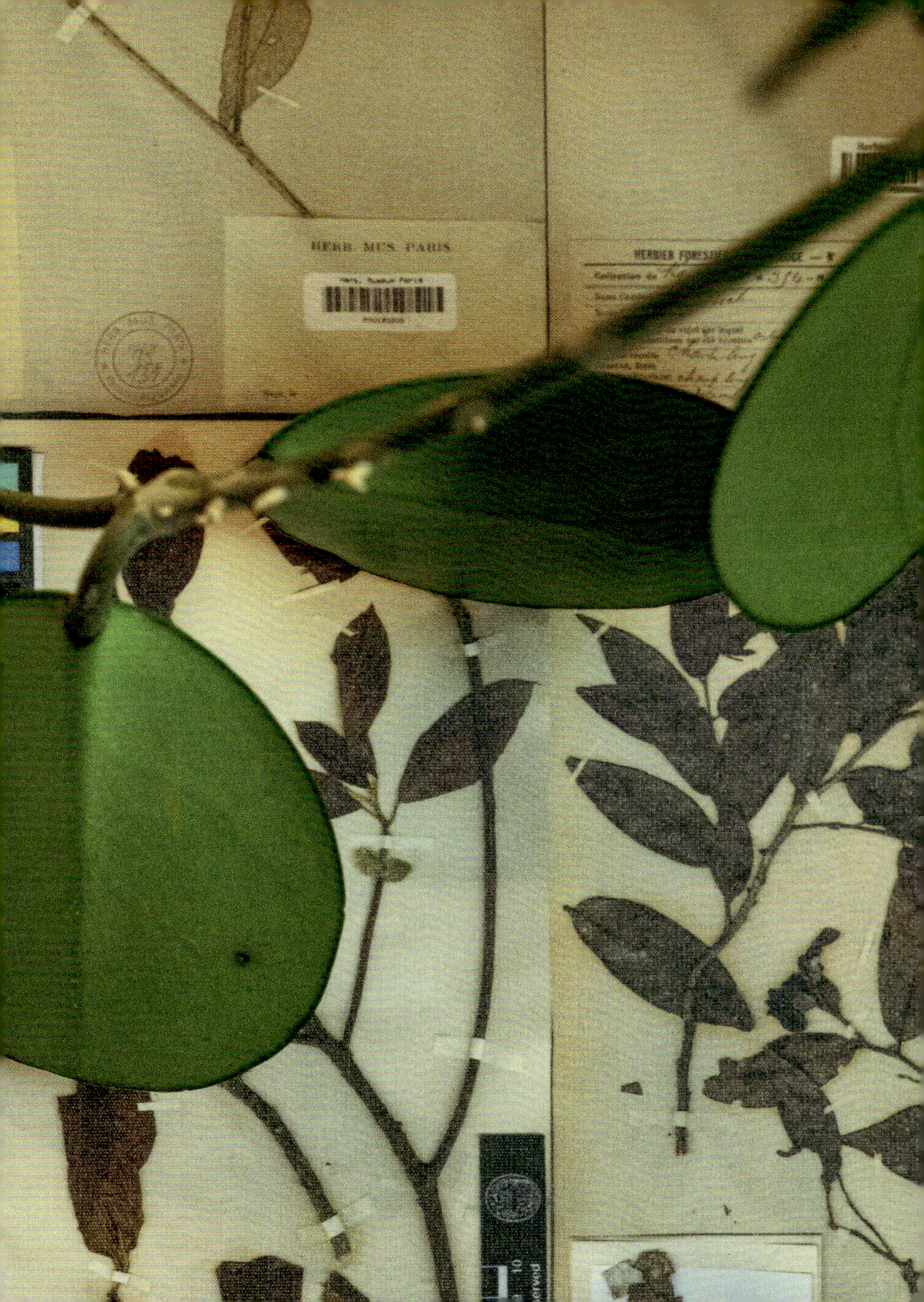
HERB. MUS. PARIS

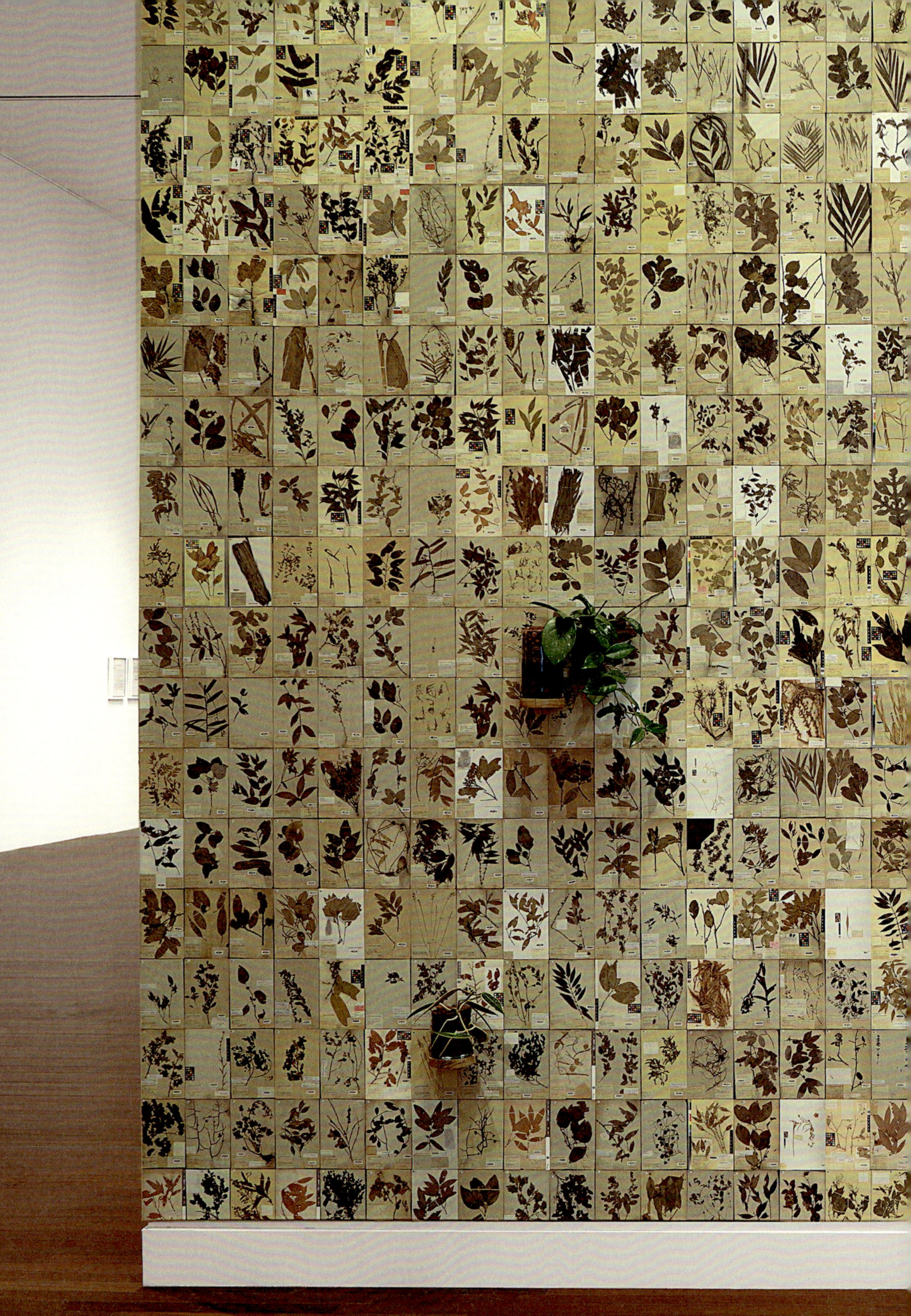

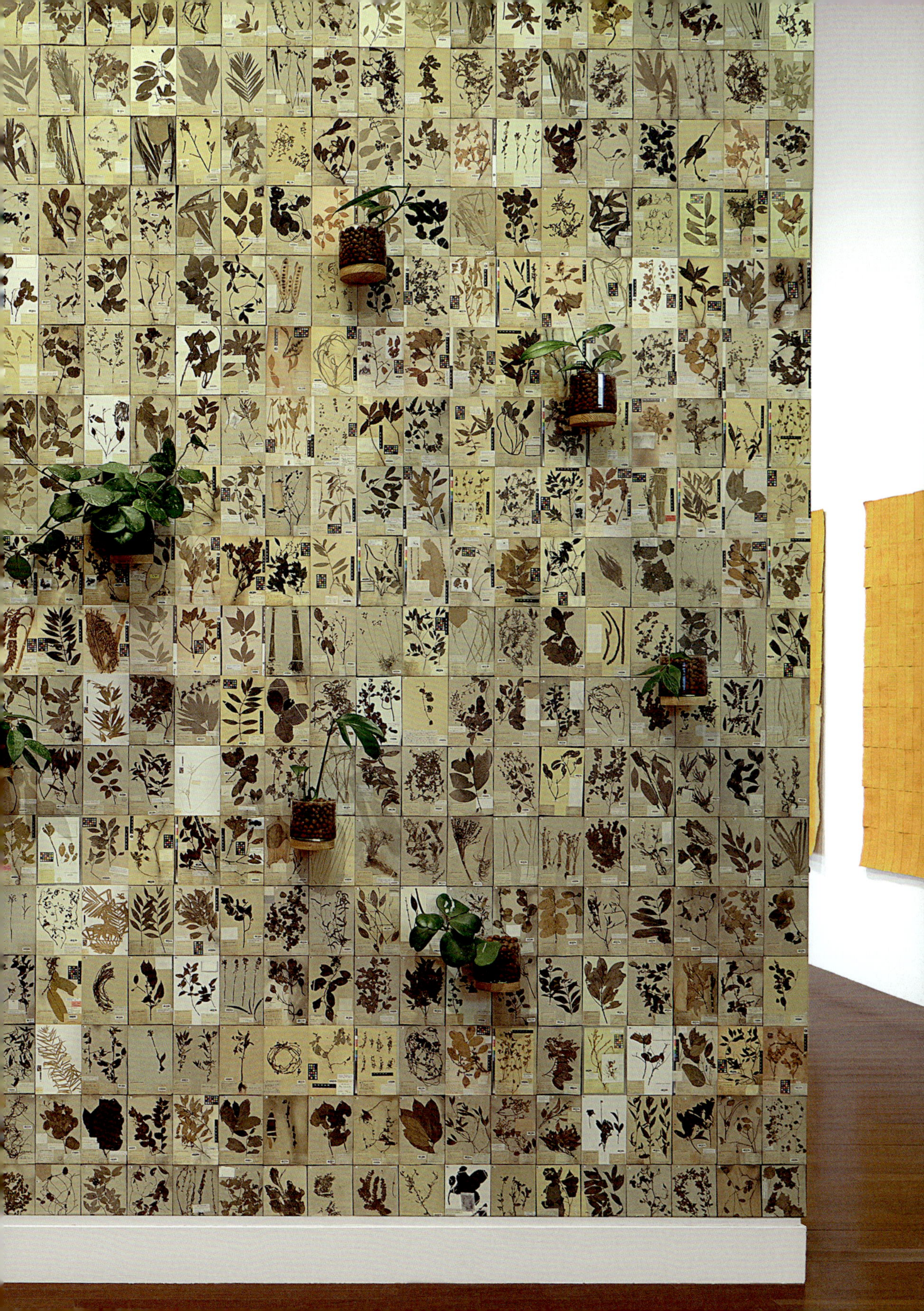

The Voice Is an Archive, 2016
Video (black and white, sound),
6 min.

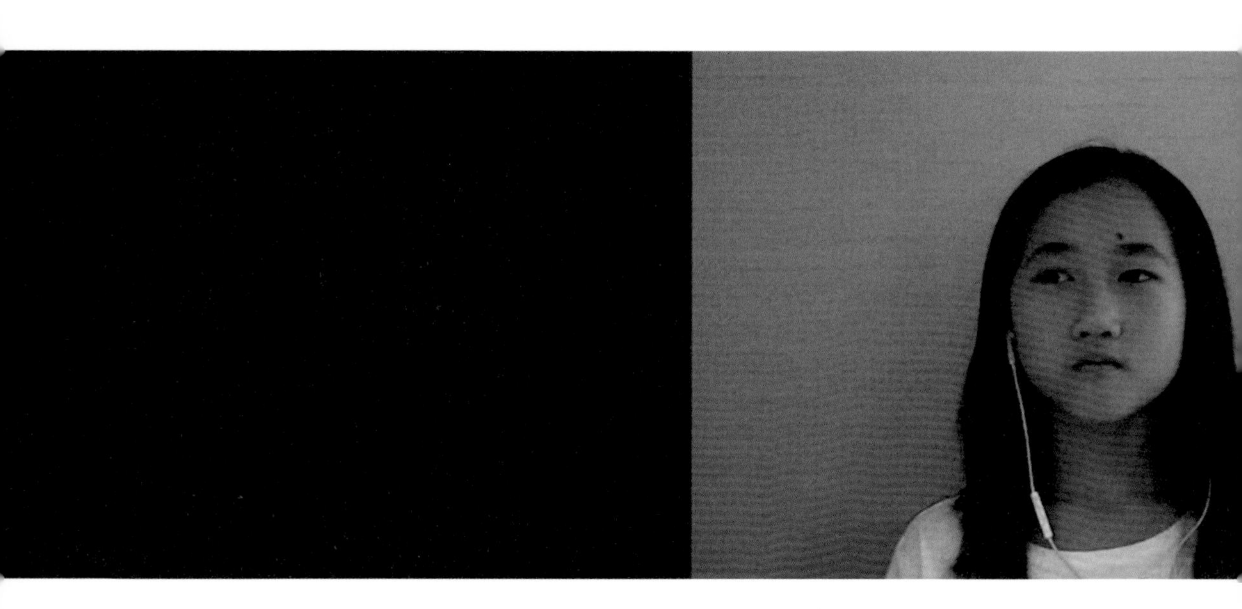

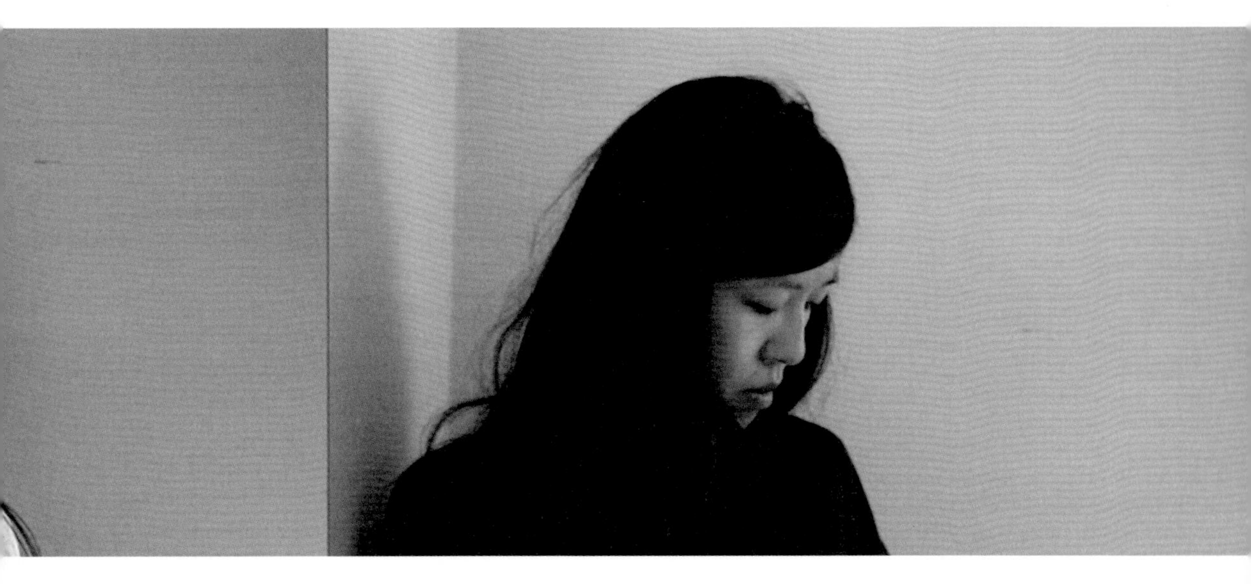

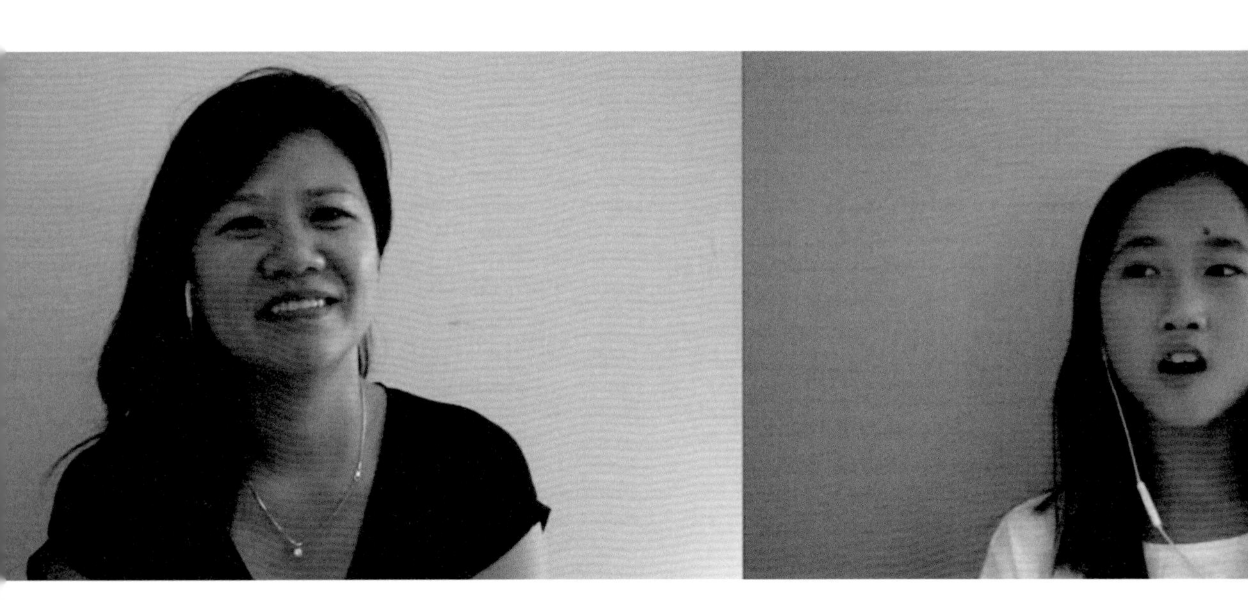

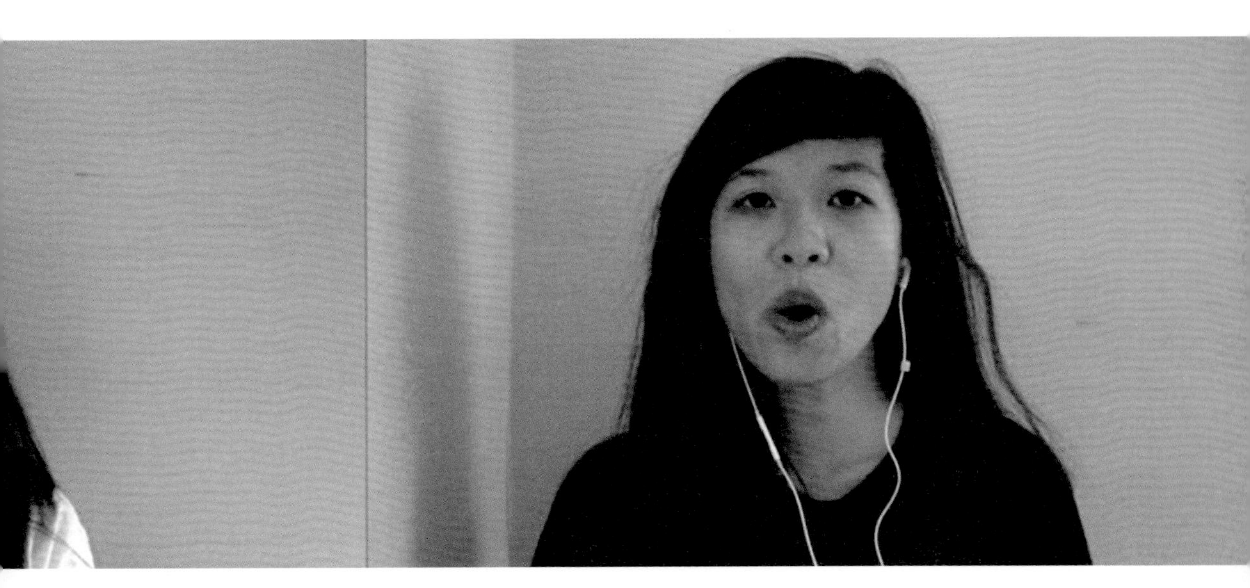

UNGRAFTING: THERE/ HERE

A CONVERSATION BETWEEN
CHADWICK ALLEN &
EVYN LÊ ESPIRITU GANDHI

CA As an intellectual orientation and practice, Indigenous studies begins with questions about location. Where are we? Whose lands and waters are we on? Whose grounded histories are we intersecting? And how might the specificity of these lands and waters and the details of these histories influence our work? How might our location, *here*, affect how we make meaning?

In my own work in Indigenous literary and cultural studies, I've tried to move away from always placing the Indigenous in relation to the colonizing culture and its aesthetic standards. What happens instead when we place Indigenous voices and perspectives and values in relation to each other? What if we organize literary, arts, cultural, and other humanities-based scholarship *across* and *among* multiple Indigenous traditions, rather than endlessly recenter colonial structures and the Indigenous-settler binary? What if we shift methodological emphasis away from an ideal of deracinated, "objective" comparison to more grounded articulations of specific and specifically routed itineraries for juxtaposition?

I developed the idea of the "trans-Indigenous" to explore both the possibilities and the many challenges—conceptual, practical, ethical—of organizing interpretive work that centers not only multiple Indigenous voices, but also multiple Indigenous epistemologies, ontologies, and relationalities.

Hương Ngô embodies a trans-Indigenous methodology by placing *Ungrafting*'s nuanced critique of French colonialism in Vietnam in purposeful relation with the exhibit's physical location in Colorado Springs. More than a set of objects on display, and more than an insider conversation, *Ungrafting* enacts ways of seeing, *from* multiple Indigenous locations and *through* multiple Indigenous perspectives.

EG I think trawns-Indigenous presents a beautiful analytic for describing how *Ungrafting* attends to place and space, people and plants, and movement and migration thereof across Vietnam and Colorado Springs. What is striking to me about Hương Ngô's exhibit is how it bears witness to not only the colonial, but also the *settler* colonial dimensions of the French occupation of Vietnam: the social and political overpowering of the ethnic Kinh majority *and* the land dispossession of Indigenous minorities, such as the Hmong, Tay, and Nùng. The emphasis on resistance embodied in the term *Ungrafting*—an act of both undoing colonial violence and creating something new in its wake—thus takes on both anticolonial and *decolonial* resonances: an aspiration for postcolonial independence but also a reminder of Indigenous communities that do not fit easily within the nation-state frame. Moreover, the exhibit takes inspiration from Indigenous studies interventions that attend to the entanglement of human-nonhuman relations across people, plants, and soil

This decolonial impetus is most apparent in *Latent Images (Grafts)* (2024). In this series, Ngô reworks early twentieth-century images that she found in the French national archives. Indexing French settler colonial logics, these prints depict foreign trees that were grafted onto native ones, with Indigenous subjects positioned nearby for scale, their presence notably absented from the colonial captions. Ngô's decolonial reworking of these prints operates via both framing and medium. By juxtaposing the images with works from Indigenous artists, notably from the Fine Arts Center's permanent collection, and red-colored soil from Colorado, the series recenters trans-Indigenous connections and invites place-based specificity. By reproducing the images using the Van Dyke method but omitting the crucial fixer, Ngô allows this colonial archive to deteriorate over time, making space for alternative relations to emerge in its wake.

CA That's a good way of putting it, a *re*centering of the Indigenous. Wherever I stood in the gallery, my eyes were drawn to the set of painted perpendicular walls in the back corner. Forming a reddish-brown square pillar, the walls anchor the exhibit space with color and texture. They evoke the presence of the distant

Red River in Vietnam, but also, as you note, Colorado ("red colored") soil. There *and* here. This simultaneity is not a superimposition, a layering of one thing over another, or even a palimpsest, but rather a purposeful juxtaposition, a *placing beside*.

The effect is subtle and complex. The west wall has been coated in the Benjamin Moore paint color *Red River Clay*, creating a matte uniform surface. The intersecting south wall, however, has been coated in layers of actual soil from Colorado, variegated and rich with iron, creating an uneven surface of clotted orange-browns and running gypsums that evoke the histories of its making—geological, but also mixed by human hand. As it dries and crusts, the wall continues to transform and change. At the corner, the convergence of the homogenized and fixed commercial product with its multicolored, multitextured, living inspiration evokes the verb *to cleave*, which means to separate but also to join. This contrast is a coming together, another articulation of grafting.

Part of the draw, for me personally, is that I come from a place that is also haunted by a Red River, the one that forms the living border between what are now the US states of Oklahoma and Texas. In the nineteenth century, the Oklahoma side was known as the Indian Territory. My family is from south-central Oklahoma, where the Chickasaw were forcibly relocated and had to remake their relations with lands-waters-skies. But another part of the draw is that the walls speak to other parts of the exhibit, creating a call and response: the stitched-together textiles streaked with iron, clay, and copper; the handmade paper, also stitched together, that evokes tree bark and both human and animal skin; the Van Dyke prints you mentioned of grafted trees posed with Indigenous people in Vietnam aglow in rich variations of sepia and ferrous red but, exposed to light and air, already transforming, already making new relations.

EG I appreciate you bringing the personal into our discussion. As the daughter and granddaughter of Vietnamese refugees situated in Tovaangar, and as a scholar working at the intersection of critical refugee studies and settler colonial studies, I am committed to asking how Vietnamese diasporic subjects can participate in projects of decolonization. This exhibit offers many generative answers, from Vietnam to Turtle Island: there *and* here, as you say.

Another key term that the exhibit calls to mind for me is translation. We can think of grafting as a form of translation or movement of plants (but also people) from one place/language/culture to another, from there to here; likewise, the "trans" in trans-Indigenous invites conversations between multiple Indigenous places and contexts. These connections are made readily apparent in *Studies for Translations* (2024). Turn a corner in the exhibit, and you are suddenly met with a startling wall of green: a marked contrast to the red, copper, and iron tones that, as you rightly note, otherwise characterize the exhibit. Reproduced images of green herbarium samples collected from the French colonies for Muséum national d'histoire naturelle in Paris present a backdrop for verdant houseplants from Ngô's own collection, some of which may have originated from French Indochina. Here, Indigenous presence is latent though stubbornly present. As the exhibit placard notes, "Even as they dispossessed Indigenous peoples of their lands, the French relied on local knowledge as they collected, systematically documented, and categorized plant specimens." Plant migrations mirror refugee migrations: displaced from Vietnam, diasporic subjects have taken root in new lands and waters, forging relations with new Indigenous communities and places.

Translation is also explicit in *We are here because you were there* (2016–ongoing), a series of hectographs printed using agar, derived from red algae (another plant), that feature variations on the phrases, "We are here because you were there" and "We are still here" in English, Vietnamese, and French. The first phrase calls out the roles French

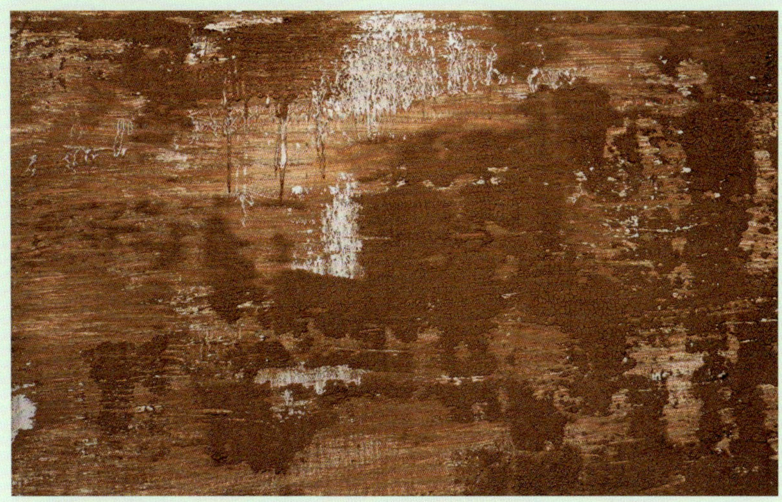

Installation detail from *Ungrafting*, 2024. Colorado Springs Fine Arts Center at Colorado College.

colonialism and US imperialism played in displacing and resettling Vietnamese refugees. The second phrase voices Indigenous defiance: an enduring presence despite settler colonial dispossession, both there and here.

Lastly, I appreciated how the placards in the exhibit appear in English, Vietnamese, and Spanish to speak to multiple audiences. Text near the beginning of the exhibit explains that Ngô and the Vietnamese translator Hùng Dương chose to translate "ungrafting" as the more poetic *phóng thích cây chủ* (to liberate the host tree) rather than the more technical *cắt cành ghép* (to cut the scion) to attend to the liberatory and decolonial dimensions of the exhibit.

CA Follow the hallway past the *We are here because you were there* installation and you reach *Affinities*, objects Ngô selected from the FAC's permanent collection. I was drawn, especially, to two of these pieces: I felt a particular energy in the space between the decorated clay storage jar from Cochiti Pueblo, artist no longer known but dated to the early nineteenth century, and the "storm pattern" woven textile by Diné artist Marilyn Jim, dated from the late twentieth century. Here is a more local call and response, clay and paint, fiber and dye, but also a hailing, a welcoming, a calling in.

EG Yes! It's a calling in that also invites an opening out, towards other Asian-Indigenous encounters and histories of transpacific migration. From the FAC's permanent collection, I was drawn to *Japanese Children's Day Carp Banners, Paguate Village, Jackpile Mine Uranium Tailings, Laguna Pueblo Reservation, New Mexico* (1990) by Patrick A. Nagatani, which layers the intersecting histories of Japanese incarceration during World War II and US mining of uranium on Laguna territory—uranium that was then used to construct the bombs dropped on Hiroshima and Nagasaki. Likewise, *Ungrafting* highlights intersecting histories and presences of refugee migration, Indigenous survivance, and decolonial ecologies, there/here.

LIST OF WORKS

We are here because you were there, 2016–ongoing
Hectograph
Courtesy the artist

To cut, to bleed, a rust-colored river, 2024
Cotton, hemp, silk, linen, copper, iron, and clay on mahogany and white oak armature
Commissioned by the Fine Arts Center at Colorado College, courtesy the artist

Latent Images (Grafts), 2024
Van Dyke prints on paper
Commissioned by the Fine Arts Center at Colorado College, courtesy the artist

In Passing I, 2017
Archival pigment print on silk habotai, custom wood armature
DePaul Art Museum, Chicago

Letter from Nguyễn Thị Minh Khai's father to Marshall Philippe Pétain, 2017
Laser-cut onion skin paper mounted on teak
Courtesy the artist

Letter from Nguyễn Thị Minh Khai to father (Nguyễn Văn Bình), 2017
Laser-cut onion skin paper mounted on teak
Courtesy the artist

Letter from Nguyễn Thị Minh Khai to Comrades or Các Anh (Brothers) (pages 1 and 2), 2017
Laser-cut onion skin paper mounted on teak
Courtesy the artist

Letters from and about agent "LESQUENDIEU," 2017
Laser-cut onion skin paper mounted on teak
Courtesy the artist

Profile of Nguyễn Thị Minh Khai (pages 1 and 2), 2017
Laser-cut onion skin paper mounted on teak
Courtesy the artist

Up Against the State, 2017
Invisible ink on paper, iodine
Courtesy the artist

Da/Skin (I, II), 2024
Stitched handmade dó paper
Courtesy the artist

Graphs, 2024
Wood, clamps, sound
Courtesy the artist

Studies for Ungrafting, 2024
Blind-embossed Rives BFK paper
Commissioned by the Fine Arts Center at Colorado College, courtesy the artist

Studies for Translations, 2024
Reproductions of herbarium specimens and plants in LECA (lightweight, expanded clay aggregate)
Courtesy the artist

The Voice Is an Archive, 2016
Video (black and white, sound), 6 min.
Courtesy the artist

FAC PERMANENT COLLECTION WORKS

Patrick Nagatani
(American, 1945–2017)
Japanese Children's Day Carp Banners, Paguate Village, Jackpile Mine Uranium Tailings, Laguna Pueblo Reservation, New Mexico, 1990
Chromogenic color print
Gift of A.E. Manley, FA 2005.18.13

Kevin Red Star
(Crow [Apsáalooke], b. 1943)
Corn Woman and Grandchildren, 1980
Lithograph
Museum Purchase, FA 1990.14.3

Unrecorded artist
(Pueblo de Cochiti)
Storage jar, ca. 1800–50
Clay, slip, paint
Gift of Alice Bemis Taylor, TM 4370

Jaune Quick-To-See Smith
(Confederated Salish and Kootenai, b. 1940)
Wallowa Water Hole Series, 1979
Lithograph
Museum Purchase, FA 1990.13.43

Andrea Chung
(American, b. 1978)
Mushroom, 2019
Cyanotype and sugar
Museum Purchase, FAC.2023.001.0001

Amado Maurilio Peña Jr.
(Pascua Yaqui, American, b. 1943)
Huelga (Strike), 1980
Serigraph
Museum Purchase, FA 1990.14.27

Marilyn Jim
(Navajo (Diné), b. 1966)
Storm pattern Diné rug, Mid- to late 20th century
Wool
Donated by Michael Ryan in memory of Sarah Ryan, FAC 2023.002.0016

Harry L. Standley
(American, 1881–1951)
Tower of Babel-Garden of the Gods, Early to mid-20th century
Black-and-white photograph
Gift of Miss Hilda Standley, FA 1951.2.57

John James Audubon
(French American, 1785–1851)
Hand-colored by Robert Havell Jr.
(American, 1793–1878)
Chestnut-Backed Titmouse, Black-capped Titmouse, Chestnut-Crowned Titmouse, 1837
Hand-colored engraving
Gift of the Estate of Phillip B Stewart, FA 1958.6.146

Hương Ngô: Ungrafting
is published by
Inventory Press
2305 Hyperion Ave
Los Angeles, CA 90027
inventorypress.com
&
Colorado Springs Fine Arts Center
at Colorado College
30 W. Dale St
Colorado Springs, CO 80903
fac.coloradocollege.edu

Copyediting and Proofreading
Eugenia Bell

Design
IN-FO.CO (Adam Michaels, V. E. Chen)

Editing
Katja Rivera

Fonts
Đanh Đá by Hương Ngô and Giang Nguyễn
Neue moderne Grotesk by Forgotten Shapes
Job Clarendon by DJR

Printed and bound in Belgium by die Keure

ISBN: 978-1-941753-65-1
LCCN: 2024940301

Distributed by
ARTBOOK | D.A.P.
75 Broad St, Suite 630
New York, NY 10004
artbook.com

Photo Credits
Photos by Stacy J Platt: pp. 7, 11, 14–15, 18–19, 96–97, 109; Jonathan Dankenbring and J. D. Sell: pp. 62–63, 72–73, 76, 98–99; Wes Magyar: pp. 9, 12–13, 16–17, 20–21, 52–53, 64–67, 70–71; Tom Van Eynde: 50–51; all other photos by the artist